S0-AIY-428

# THE AQUARIAN

# I CHING

# THE AQUARIAN
# I CHING

## MARSHALL PEASE

BROTHERHOOD OF LIFE, INC.
ALBUQUERQUE, NEW MEXICO

©1993 Marshall Pease
First printing – 1993
Published by Brotherhood of Life, Inc.
110 Dartmouth, SE
Albuquerque, NM 87106-2218

All rights reserved. No part of this publication may be reproduced or transmitted in any form or by any means, electronic or mechanical, including photocopy, without permission in writing from Brotherhood of Life, Inc. Reviewers may quote brief passages.

ISBN 0-914732-30-7

Typeset in Galliard and Charlegmane
Printed on Recycled paper with Soy ink
PRINTED IN THE UNITED STATES OF AMERICA

# CONTENTS

## LIST OF TABLES AND FIGURES

# PREFACE

Within the dualities of existence there is the monality of reality, but only at the ultimate center. The center is concealed within a vast nesting of contingent polarities. As each layer is peeled away, only a new layer is found and the jewel within the lotus remains in ultimate concealment. Yet it is the jewel that is sought by the seeker and is the aim and purpose of the Path, and there is no other goal worth seeking. The leaves of the lotus are death in its myriad variety, and only the jewel is life. Yet even the deaths are but pauses upon the Path for the Path must be trod; there is no other way. Death is but an agony to drive the spirit on. The soul may wander in the maze of deaths and dwindle toward extinction. Yet, in the end if it is not to be scattered as dust among the stars, it must take up the staff and seek not the agonies of death but the trials of the Path, which are the agonies of life. It will find that which it seeks, if not now, then later. In the finding, it will become.

# CHAPTER I

# INTRODUCTION

This chapter sets the stage for our study of the I Ching, the ancient Chinese book of divination and wisdom. In it, the scope and purpose of the book are discussed. In it also, the reader is introduced to the I Ching through a brief summary of its history and a short description of its use and interpretation. In the next chapter we consider divination in greater depth—what it is, why it can be valuable, and what approach to it is appropriate. Subsequent chapters, then, concentrate on the I Ching's symbolism, our main theme.

## INTENTION

It may seem presumptuous to offer a new interpretation of the I Ching. It is a book of wisdom sanctified by age-long use (at least 31 centuries) and by the labor of many very wise men; who am I to tamper with it? Nevertheless, Chinese tradition allows for new interpretations and commentaries. Indeed, almost all Chinese philosophers have added their own contributions. It is quite in accord with tradition to offer my own.

The I Ching *is* open to new interpretation—perhaps more so than almost any similar material or divinatory technique. By its nature it must be, for it uses what should probably be regarded as archetypal images—no doubt one reason why the I Ching has remained valid and useful even after some 31 centuries and across a vast cultural gap. Archetypal images cannot be exactly defined or even fully identified— that is what makes them archetypal—but must be interpreted in relation to some context. The basic images of the I Ching will always require adaptation to the user's society and background, and to the particular situation.

The I Ching tradition also recognizes the need to interpret its answers according to the question and the questioner; it does not claim to be a system that can be applied blindly, without intuition. The Chinese word *Ling* describes the ability to use the I Ching for divination; it is recognized as having two components: the ability to obtain a meaningful answer to a question by one of the techniques described later and then the ability to see what that answer has to do with the question. The latter component implies the need for intuition and its use to interpret the text according to the needs of the questioner.

Having claimed a right to offer my own commentary, I must also enter a disclaimer. It is not my intention to create text that can replace the original or that can serve all the needs of our present age and society. I do not mean to replace *any* of the older wisdom, but to augment it. Further, this work is developed from a fairly specialized viewpoint. Its interpretation, therefore, should be used only when it applies, not forced blindly onto all problems. I hope it will be found applicable and useful in areas that are important; I do not expect it to answer all problems.

This work has another purpose, also, which derives from seeing the I Ching as an "algebra" of human interaction with the world around us. By this I mean that the I Ching provides a self-consistent and powerful framework that allows us to classify our interactions, and allows us to examine some of the implications of a particular kind of interaction. The generality of the framework makes it largely archetypal in nature, and so beyond what can be fully understood by discursive analysis. The way to study it, therefore, is to consider particular contexts, seeking to see beyond the limits of the context. This implies the need to study the I Ching in a frame of reference that is relevant to modern life. It is my hope that this work will be a useful step in that direction to others as well as to myself.

The view of the I Ching as a more or less archetypal analysis of a person's place in the world has further implications about how it should be studied. As suggested, its ultimate wisdom cannot be grasped by the intellect alone; it must be used. This suggests that the student should develop his or her own viewpoint and interpretation— or interpretations—and that this effort is a necessary part of assimilating the underlying wisdom. I hope, therefore, that this book will be useful in showing students one way of moving toward their own views, and that it will encourage them to do so.

In the hope, then, that the work will prove useful in a variety of ways, we will now turn to the I Ching itself.

# HISTORICAL PERSPECTIVE

The history of the I Ching is most impressive; few other systems of thought can claim either its duration of continual usage or its links to other religious or philosophical systems. We will not attempt to give a complete account here; the interested reader can find considerable additional information in many other texts. But we do want to sketch in some of its historical context, enough to orient readers who may have little or no previous knowledge of the I Ching.

As stated, the I Ching is an ancient Chinese book of wisdom and divination. The title itself means *Book of Change* or *Book of Changes*—the Chinese language does not distinguish, and either would be appropriate.

The main part of the original text is attributed to King Wen, the founder of the Chou dynasty, and is considered to have been written around 1150 B.C. King Wen is said to have written it while incarcerated by Chou Hsin, the tyrant he later overthrew. The other part of the original text, that on the individual lines,[1] is attributed to the Duke of Chou, King Wen's son. He is said to have been under house arrest, also at the orders of Chou Hsin, when he wrote the material.

So the text we have is ancient—about 31 centuries old. Further, there exist fragments of an earlier text which is claimed to have been written in the Hsia dynasty (traditionally 2205–1766 B.C.). This text apparently recognized the trigrams but listed the hexagrams in a different sequence than King Wen's. Still a third version is mentioned by Confucius, one supposedly written during the Shang dynasty (traditionally 1766–1150 B.C.). So, the I Ching in its various versions is ancient, indeed.

---

1. What is meant by the lines and, later, the trigrams and hexagrams, will be described shortly.

The version that we have, King Wen's, predates both Confucius and Taoism, and has connections to both. Confucius lived in about the seventh century B.C., roughly five centuries after King Wen, and is known to have been a student of the I Ching. Either he or his followers wrote a series of commentaries known as the *Ten Wings* that are accepted as part of the canonical literature on the I Ching.

There is a story—it is probably no more than that—that Confucius at the age of 70 said he wished he could live fifty more years. According to the tale, he added that if he could, he would spend those years studying the I Ching and then might not make so many mistakes. The story is almost certainly apocryphal, but it does suggest the depth of his connection with the I Ching—or the depth ascribed to him by his followers.

There is also a link between the I Ching and Taoism. Taoism started sometime before 700 B.C., perhaps in the ninth century B.C. Lao Tse, the traditional if somewhat misty founder of Taoism (even his existence is uncertain), is also supposed to have been a student of the I Ching. Whether this is so or what direct connection there was between the early Taoists and the I Ching is uncertain. However, it is very difficult to talk about, or use, the I Ching without using Taoist concepts and terms like *yin* and *yang*—words that did not exist in the Chinese language in the time of King Wen. There is certainly a strong commonality of viewpoint; the two approaches must have had at least common intellectual roots.

It can be said, therefore, that the I Ching lies at the foundation of two of the major religions of the world, Taoism and Confucianism. Few other books can even begin to approach those credentials.

The I Ching has remained in use in most of the Orient up to and during modern times. It has remained a vital and viable system for many people living in many different cultures over a tremendous span of time.

The I Ching's history in the West is considerably shorter, but even its history in the West is not negligible. The earliest generally available translation into a Western language was by James Legge, published originally in 1882 as Vol. XVI in his series titled *The Sacred Books of the East*. It is currently available from Dover Publications, Inc., New York, NY. There were earlier translations, also, but these are not generally available. The translation which many people consider the standard was written by Richard Wilhelm in the German language and translated into English by Cary F. Baynes. The English version was first published as *The I Ching or Book of Changes* in the Bollingen Series XIX, by Princeton University Press, Princeton, NJ, in 1950. (This work contains a most interesting and insightful Foreword by Carl G. Jung.) Another translation that is worth particular mention is that by John Blofeld titled *The Book of Change,* published by E. P. Dutton and Co., Inc., New York, NY, in 1966. Other, more recent translations have also been published and can contribute to understanding—this is not intended as an exhaustive list. The main point that is significant here is that the I Ching has been of persistent interest to many people in the West ever since it first became available.

So what is the I Ching that it has excited such persistent interest? Most obviously, it is a system of divination. It is also a book of wisdom, implicitly expressing a world view. Finally and perhaps most usefully, it is a training tool for the intuition. It is worthy of study, not only for its use as a tool of divination (or even despite it, if the idea of divination be dismissed as superstition), but because study of it can open new paths for growth within the practitioner.

## THE HEXAGRAMS

The I Ching in King Wen's version is a collection of short readings associated with what are called *hexagrams,* plus a second set of readings associated with the individual lines. So we must understand what a hexagram is, and what are its lines.

A hexagram is a figure composed of six lines, each of which is either broken or solid. For example, the third hexagram in the sequence, called "Difficulty at the Beginning," is the figure shown in Figure 1. The numbers on the left indicate how the individual lines are designated—i.e., from the bottom up. This is a point that can cause confusion and should be carefully noted. In "Difficulty at the Beginning," therefore, the first and fifth lines are solid, the rest broken:

The various hexagrams describe, in symbolic terms, ways in which persons can interact with the world around them, particularly with those aspects of the world that pose challenges or problems. The meanings assigned to the hexagrams, and the logic that leads to them,

Figure 1

| THE HEXAGRAM "DIFFICULTY AT THE BEGINNING" | |
| --- | --- |
| 6 | ▬▬  ▬▬ |
| 5 | ▬▬▬▬▬ |
| 4 | ▬▬  ▬▬ |
| 3 | ▬▬  ▬▬ |
| 2 | ▬▬  ▬▬ |
| 1 | ▬▬▬▬▬ |

are, of course, among the main theme of this work. At this point, we will simply note that, since each line can be either solid or broken and since there are six lines in a hexagram, the number of different hexagrams—and so the number of types of situations they identify—is $2 \times 2 \times 2 \times 2 \times 2 \times 2 = 64$. The process of "casting the oracle," described later, is a technique that leads to the selection of a particular one of these hexagrams as the answer to a question.

This is not the end, however. The process generates what we call the primary hexagram. In addition, the process may identify some of the lines in the primary hexagram as changing. How many and which lines are changing is determined by the process itself—no lines may be changing, or all of them, or any number in between. If there are changing lines, a secondary hexagram is obtained by changing all the changing lines. That is, if a changing line was broken, it is now made solid; if it was solid, it is now made broken. The lines that are not changing are left unchanged—i.e., solid or broken as in the primary hexagram. This mechanism allows a given primary hexagram to change into any other hexagram if it has the appropriate number and pattern of changing lines.

To illustrate: suppose the primary hexagram is Difficulty at the Beginning, as shown in Figure 1. Suppose also that the process led to the 5th and 6th lines being identified as changing (remembering to count from the bottom). In Figure 2, we indicate this by putting an x alongside the changing lines in the primary hexagram. When we change these lines, the fifth line becomes a broken one, and the sixth line a solid one. The result is a new hexagram—in this case the one called "The Corners of the Mouth" or "Nourishment," also shown in Figure 2.

Figure 2

| AN EXAMPLE OF CHANGING LINES | | |
|---|---|---|
| PRIMARY | CHANGES TO | SECONDARY |
| ✗ ▬▬ ▬▬ | ——————▶ | ▬▬▬▬▬ |
| ✗ ▬▬▬▬▬ | ——————▶ | ▬▬ ▬▬ |
| ▬▬ ▬▬ | | ▬▬ ▬▬ |
| ▬▬ ▬▬ | | ▬▬ ▬▬ |
| ▬▬ ▬▬ | | ▬▬ ▬▬ |
| ▬▬▬▬▬ | | ▬▬▬▬▬ |
| #3 Difficulty at the Beginning | | #27 Corners of the Mouth (Nourishment) |

Both of these hexagrams are used in answering the question. Their separate significances are discussed later. The numbers before their names, #3 and #27, indicate their positions in the sequence of hexagrams and are used as indices to the hexagrams.

Since there are 64 different hexagrams and each hexagram can change into any other or not change at all, there are a total of 64 x 64 = 4096 distinct answers possible. The procedure that is used, however, makes many of the combinations unlikely. On average, there will be no changing lines about 17.8% of the time, one changing line about 35.6%, two about 29.7%, three about 13.2%, four about 3.3%, five about 0.4%, and six about once in 5000 times. So, we mostly get no changing lines or one or two and there are more than two changing lines only about one time in six. This still leaves enough possibilities to allow for a considerable range of answers.

# THE PROCESS OF "CASTING THE ORACLE"

There are two common methods used for "casting the oracle"—i.e., for using the I Ching to answer a question. The older one uses a set of dried yarrow stalks which are manipulated in a complicated and somewhat tedious way to generate the answer. The other method is to throw three coins simultaneously six times. Since I have not discovered any substantial difference in quality between the two methods, I will discuss only the coin method, which is considerably simpler and faster than the other.

It is worth noting that the two methods are not exactly equivalent, even in probabilistic terms. They both lead to equal probabilities that a given line is solid or broken. They both also lead to a 25% chance that a particular line is changing. In the yarrow-stalk method, however, the probability that a line is changing is somewhat different according to whether it is solid or broken. With the coins, there is no difference. The effect is not large, but it is not entirely insignificant. Nevertheless, the coin method seems entirely satisfactory, and is certainly easier and quicker (though speed may not be an advantage!)[2].

In the coin method, we start with the coins themselves. Many people prefer to use Chinese coins, arguing that they are appropriate to a Chinese system. My own preference is for American coins on the basis that my subconscious is well trained in them. My only recommendation is that a person use what feels right to him or her.

Given that coins have been chosen, one side is designated as the yang or strong side, the other as the yin or weak side.[3] Traditionally, if Chinese coins are used, the side with the Chinese characters is the yin side. (A few Chinese coins have characters on both sides, in which

---

2. For instructions using the "yarrow-stalk" method, consult the Wilhelm/
Baynes *I Ching*, published by Princeton University Press.
3. As has been indicated, the terms yang and yin are Taoist terms that were not in the language at the time of King Wen. They are convenient, however, and it seems awkward, and somewhat pedantic, to avoid their use. We will be flexible and will use them without apology or further note when convenient.

case a decision must be made.) My own rule for American coins is to take heads as yang, tails as yin. This is consistent with the Chinese coins since the characters on the latter indicate the coin's value and the value of an American coin is given on the tails side. Again, however, you should use whatever convention feels right. It is only important that you be very clear in your own mind what convention you are using.

The side of the coin designated as yin is assigned the value 2, the yang side 3. What happened to the number 1? It is the symbol of the unity before duality, and the I Ching addresses the world of duality. Therefore the number 1 is not used.[4]

In developing the primary hexagram, the three coins are thrown simultaneously six times, once for each line. Having thrown the three coins, we add their values (2 or 3) to obtain the value of the line (6, 7, 8, or 9). If the line's value is even (6 or 8), the throw is a yin throw and the line is a broken one. If the value is odd (7 or 9), the throw is a yang one and the line is solid. If the throw is a 6 or 9—i.e., all 2's or all 3's, all heads or all tails—the line is changing. As in Figure 2, a changing line is indicated by putting an x alongside it, but any systematic procedure will do.

The whole process is summarized in Table 1 on the following page. In the first column, the coins are listed as T or H—i.e., tails or heads, although the significant aspect is, of course, whether the side showing is the yin or yang side. The second column shows that the values of the coins are added to give the value of the line in the third column. The resulting line is solid or broken, and changing or not, as indicated in the fourth and last column.

The reader is reminded again that the lines are numbered from the bottom up, and are developed in the same way. The first throw of the three coins develops line #1 at the bottom of the hexagram; the second throw results in line #2 next to the bottom, and so on, for six throws.

Having thrown the coins six times and developed the primary hexagram, we then write the secondary hexagram (if there are any

---

4. It is worth noting that the yin aspect—traditionally called female—is closer to the primal monality than the yang. Since the culture out of which the I Ching arose was what we would now consider highly sexist, the implication that the female aspect is more fundamental than the male is very interesting....

**Table 1**

| EVALUATING A THROW OF THE COINS | | | | |
|---|---|---|---|---|
| THROW | VALUES OF THE COINS | VALUE OF THE LINE | LINE | CHANGING |
| T, T, T | 2 + 2 + 2 | 6 | — — | Yes (✗) |
| T, T, H | 2 + 2 + 3 | 7 | —— | No |
| T, H, H | 2 + 3 + 3 | 8 | — — | No |
| H, H, H | 3 + 3 + 3 | 9 | —— | Yes (✗) |

changing lines) by changing any lines that have been marked according to the last column in the table given above. This process is illustrated in Figure 2.

Once the primary and secondary hexagrams have been developed, they must be identified. This identification is conveniently accomplished using the chart "Key to the Hexagrams" found at the end of this book. For each hexagram, we pick the column according to the outer trigram—the top three lines of the hexagram—and the row labeled by the inner trigram—the bottom three lines. The number of the hexagram is shown at the intersection of the column and row. With the number, we can find the name from Table 5 in Key to the Hexagrams or go directly to the text.

Having completed this process, we are ready to address interpreting the results. We have completed the mechanical part of casting the I Ching. Before taking up the issue of interpretation, however, it is appropriate to consider first the nature of divination and of the world view embodied in the I Ching.

# CHAPTER II

# DIVINATION

Here, we consider the nature and purpose of divination and why it is a useful area of endeavor. At the end of the last chapter, the mechanics of casting the oracle were described. Now we begin to approach the deeper questions of why we should want to cast it at all, and what we may hope to achieve by doing so.

## VALIDITY AND VALUE

When we consider divination, whether with the I Ching or any other tool, we are inevitably faced with the question of its validity and value. How can divination work? And even if it does work, does it profit us to know the answers it gives us?

As to the how, I have mixed feelings. I am reluctant to accept the notion of a system that can predict the future, or even provide deep insights into an immediate problem. Yet it seems to. One cannot use the I Ching very long without being impressed with the results.

Carl Jung found in the I Ching an expression of what he called *synchronicity.* This viewpoint starts from the idea that reality is a single whole. The I Ching, therefore, coexists with the problem under concern and since they share the same universe they are linked one to the other. So also are my actions as I throw the coins. Hence, Jung argues, it may not be entirely surprising that, to some degree and in some way, the throw of the coins is linked to the problem. Neither exists independently of the other, and each can, logically, affect the other.

As an exercise in logic, the connection does certainly exist. However, the coexistence of a problem and the act of throwing the coins in the same universe does not seem to offer any explanation of how the connection can lead to consequences that I can interpret as helping me find an answer to my question.

The counter theory is that the answers are, in fact, no more than coincidentally relevant. This view would argue that any insights gained through use of the I Ching would depend entirely on the user, not at all on the I Ching itself. That explanation would satisfy the scientist in me; unfortunately, it does not seem to fit my experience. I am left without any very good way of explaining the I Ching's relevance, yet am unable to deny the relevance that experience with the I Ching has apparently demonstrated.

As a scientist, I would like to conduct some controlled experiments with the I Ching. This does not seem feasible because of the nature of the I Ching itself. To illustrate, we might run a series of questions on whether or not it will rain tomorrow, expecting to be able to compile some meaningful statistics. The difficulty with such an experiment, however, is that the I Ching can often be seen to respond to the underlying question, not the one the questioner claims to be asking. In a sequence of "is it going to rain?" questions, the underlying question would be how the I Ching was going to respond to the test; the question about raining is irrelevant. Therefore, we might properly expect an answer that referred to the experimenters' attitude, perhaps telling us to get lost or that our experiment is worthless. (For example, one might get the hexagram called *Youthful Folly!* I have seen this hexagram returned to people who asked what might well be called impertinent questions!) The I Ching represents a point of view that is basically antipathetic to the objectivity required of scientific studies.

The I Ching reflects a mode of thought that is often overlooked or disregarded in western thought. This was also noted by Carl Jung; we might call the mode the *synchronistic* one. In this view, events are conceived as arising out of the whole matrix of experience and current existence. They are seen as consequences of the entire state of the universe, not merely of certain aspects labeled causes. This contrasts with the dominant western, scientific mode that isolates particular aspects to the exclusion of all others, calling them the causes of the event. The latter mode can be called *causal* or *linear*.

To illustrate the difference in these modes of thinking, suppose I hit a baseball and ask why the ball travels as it does. If the question is taken in the causal sense, it is answered by discussing the laws of motion and the physical properties of the bat and ball. If it is taken in the synchronistic sense, the answer must take account of why I am there trying to hit the ball, and why I succeed. Two very different questions are involved, even though they use the same words.

Both modes are needed—and used—in our culture, but we tend to be much more aware of the causal mode, and to ignore the times we use the synchronistic one. For example, when the highway department builds a bridge across a river, it uses the full power of the causal mode in the design of that bridge. This is necessary so that we, the taxpayers and bridge-users, can be confident that the bridge will stand. However, when that department, or others, is trying to decide whether to build the bridge at all, or exactly where, the synchronistic mode is needed. The bridge, if built, will have all sorts of consequences for the people living in the neighborhood. It will alter the traffic flows in and through the area. It will link the two sides of the river, allowing people and goods to flow freely between them. It may very well change where and how the area will develop. It may alter the whole course of local history over a time period measured in decades or even centuries. The decision, therefore, should be made only after considering all the ways the bridge will interact with its environment—a statement of the problem that clearly requires a synchronistic type of approach.

The I Ching largely reflects the synchronistic mode. It implies that there is no single answer to a particular type of problem. The same question, asked by two different people or even by one person at two different times, can indeed lead to different answers—the words of the question may be the same, the external and internal environments of the question are not. Each situation, each question or instance of a question, must be approached in its own reality, including the inner reality of the person asking the question.

Given this basis, the question of how the I Ching works ceases to be approachable, or even particularly important. A scientific test implies an objectivity that is intrinsic to the causal viewpoint, but contradictory to the synchronistic one. In the latter view that is so fundamental to the I Ching, the question of how becomes irrelevant or meaningless. The I Ching must be considered within its own world-view or metaphysics, and evaluated according to its own criteria of validity.

The effectiveness of the I Ching depends, in part, on this metaphysics: it tends to lead questioners to examine our problems from a perspective that is unfamiliar, yet that is at least as valid as our usual one. This new perspective may help us find a new insight into our problems. Even when we fail to find (or understand) an answer that fits what we can assimilate, we may be helped to find a new way to see our problems and the reality behind them. The I Ching is a book of wisdom; we are exposed to that wisdom whenever we try to use it.

Another approach to the question of how the I Ching can offer useful answers is in the thought that it really does not give answers at all. One way of seeing what the I Ching does is to say that it offers not answers but insight into the questioner's real problem. The implication is that the question is a problem only because the questioner is not looking at the true issue; if we can discover what our problem *really* is, we will know what to do about it. Since we may be avoiding the real question because it would be painful, the I Ching can be a harsh master. Its messages can force us to look at ourselves, for example, when we would much rather blame others for our difficulties. Denying us that escape can be painful. Yet the reality not only allows us to see what we may have to do in the immediate situation, it helps strengthen us for other challenges in the future. The I Ching can be a harsh master, but it is also an effective one.

In any case, regardless of how it functions, the I Ching is a book that has immense potential value. It depends on the students whether they will find that value. The book can be a harsh taskmaster, but, if the students are willing, they can learn from it.

# DIVINATION VERSUS FORTUNE-TELLING

We have spoken of the use of the I Ching for *divination*. In using this term, we are implying a sharp distinction from fortune-telling. It is worth being as explicit as possible about this distinction.

In fortune-telling, as I understand the term, the individual looks to be told what will happen. The questioner seeks to know how to escape his or her problem or how it will resolve. The implication is that there is nothing the questioner can or should do about it and has no responsibility for what may or will happen. It tends to be, in fact, a convenient way to get rid of an uncomfortable responsibility.

In divination, on the other hand, again as I mean the term, the individual wants to know what is going on and what are the options. There is a willingness to take full responsibility. Ideally, in fact, divination offers the means of increasing a sense of responsibility for one's self.

To illustrate, suppose I go to a fortune teller in desperate need of money. I may be told that I am about to come into an unexpected inheritance or will receive an unexpected sum from some other source. All I can do is wait for this happy (!) event, and hope that it comes true in time for my needs.

If I take the same problem to a diviner, I might be told that I am being held back by false pride, and that I should be willing to be helped. Or, I might be scolded for being greedy and told I still have something to learn from poverty. The answer is likely to emphasize the misconceptions or false self-images that have created the problem for me or have prevented my finding my own way to solve it. It is likely to point out that it is these lies and illusions that need my immediate attention. The answer may not be at all comfortable! It may dump the responsibility squarely back in my lap!

This leads to the thought that we should not ask the I Ching fortune-telling questions—those that ask for a prediction. They tend to involve at least a *de facto* avoidance of responsibility. If I am truly worried about some possible future event and seeking to consider it responsibly, my worry is in present time. Therefore the question can be rephrased to ask what should be my present attitude toward that possible future. What should I do about it, now? Maybe there are things I can do now to affect what may happen. Maybe I should take measures to guard against a possible unhappy or unfortunate future.

Put this way, the question is no longer a fortune-telling one.

More likely, questions about a future I cannot control are really intended as a test of the I Ching. If I ask about tomorrow's weather, I am probably really testing the I Ching's precognitive powers. It is likely to respond with the back of the hand—see the earlier discussion of scientific (i.e., objective) tests of the I Ching. The touchstone is, again, the issue of responsibility. While asking such a question may be intended as an expression of my responsibility as a scientist, the question itself is not one for which I have responsibility—at least as long as I am not a weather forecaster.

A more practical reason for avoiding fortune-telling questions is that the truly interesting examples of precognitive answers cannot usually be interpreted until well after the event. They are the answers that foreshadow events that are very unlikely to be guessed before the fact. The results may provide impressive examples of the power of the I Ching (I have seen such examples) but are apt to be quite useless for prediction.

So it is generally well to avoid fortune-telling questions. Instead, the more productive questions are those that call for divination concerning the present, and that express the search for understanding and responsibility.

## ASKING QUESTIONS

There are some additional rules about what kinds of questions should or should not be asked that generally apply—rules beyond the one against fortune-telling questions cited above.

The basic principle is that the question should seek to expand the questioner's sense of responsibility. Responsibility, here, means the ability to respond, or to reply. It therefore involves being willing to see and understand and act according to the present reality. It is taking on yourself the burden and the opportunity of the present. It means avoiding the blind application of past experiences as a way to bypass the need for thought or for acknowledging self-fault and error. It is *not* guilt—guilt tends to be the last refuge of those who would avoid responsibility. To feel guilty is to be absorbed in what is past, even though the consequent agony is in the present. To be responsible is to acknowledge the past, and to learn from it, and so to see the present more clearly because of past experiences.

The I Ching should not be used as a crutch to avoid responsibility. I have known people who would hardly boil an egg for breakfast without throwing the coins. This is ridiculous and a denial of the I Ching's values. The I Ching should be used as a help toward the understanding that will lead to effective decision, not as a way to dodge the need for decision.

One application of this principle is that, if the question concerns decision or action, it should be my decision, my action. Further, the decision should be of some importance to me. Or, if it involves a group action, I should be part of the group, and I should expect to play some part in forming the group's decision. In any case, the answer should involve me in some nontrivial way. To ask what somebody else should do is not my business. To ask why somebody else did something, or failed to do something, is to ask the I Ching to be a gossip. More particularly, such a question does not concern anything that is my responsibility.

If I am truly concerned about somebody else, I can, of course, ask how I should feel about what they did or did not do, or how I should respond to them. But this turns the question back toward me. Furthermore, even with this question, I should be prepared to be told to keep out of something that is not my business.

Within the scope of my own decisions or actions, the possibilities I am weighing should be ethical. Whose ethics? Mine, of course! In fact, the problem may be to discover what my own ethics are, and to separate them from those that others have imposed on me.

In other words, do not ask the I Ching whether you should rob a bank or not—at least unless you actually do think robbing a bank would be an ethical action.

Ethics are of vital importance for a quite simple reason. The only reason to ask about doing something I consider unethical is to avoid being responsible for an unethical act I want to do. In order to justify to myself doing something unethical, I must find some way to feel it is not my fault. I may tell myself I am being forced into being unethical by factors outside my control. I may argue that I am justified because I have been treated so unfairly, putting the blame on these others who, I claim, have mistreated me. I may figure out some other ingenious argument. In any case, I am seeking some way to not be responsible for my act, and asking the I Ching to help me convince myself I am not really responsible. This is counter to the whole concept of the I Ching.

Earlier, *Ling* was mentioned, the Chinese word for the ability to use the I Ching. It is said that the misuse of the I Ching diminishes *Ling*, its proper use increases *Ling*, and that which is proper or not is defined by ethics. The reason is clear. To the extent that *Ling* depends on the intuitive powers, it depends on openness, and a willingness to learn and experience. The effort to justify an unethical act (one which the doer knows is wrong) can only succeed by denying some area of experience. It requires a narrowing of the vision, a shutting down of awareness, an unwillingness to learn and experience. Therefore, a person who acts against their own concept of virtue and rightness will lose *Ling*. The I Ching demands a willingness to be responsible. In turn, it is a tool for helping the seeker toward a deeper understanding of the nature of responsibility.

## ASKING NONQUESTIONS

It is worth adding some further thoughts on the subject of divination. It is possible to use the I Ching without a specific question. Some students of the I Ching throw the coins without a question, seeking material for meditation.

In a group I ran for some time, we often asked an "unquestion" toward the end of the evening, seeking a sort of summary sermon. This developed after we had observed that the answers to various questions asked during a single evening often seemed to have a general theme. (There was one notable session that came to be known as the "humility evening.") This raised the possibility of reaching for the theme without the intervening topical questions.

I believe unquestions are useful, although their use poses some danger. In particular, it is easy to nod sagely at the answer and do nothing about it. The asking of a daily question, for example, can degenerate into something as trivial as reading the daily astrological squib in the paper.

Again the issue is one of responsibility. If I take responsibility for what the I Ching provides, using it perhaps as a seed for serious meditation, it is fine. It becomes a powerful tool for personal seeking. If I merely acknowledge it without giving it serious attention, perhaps it does no harm, but it is hard to see how it can do much good.

So, I do not try to assert a general rule, here. Again the users must do what seems right to them, even as they take responsibility for decisions to ask unquestions or not.

# CHAPTER III

# THE I CHING'S PERSPECTIVE

We can begin, now, to consider the basis of the I Ching, and to develop the detailed viewpoint that it embodies and encodes. At the same time, we can begin to relate that viewpoint to the structure of the I Ching and the symbology of its hexagrams and trigrams.

## FLOWS OF INFLUENCE

The most general statement of the I Ching's perspective seems to be that it categorizes situations according to the existing flows of influence. If I am worried about a problem, there is something in my environment that is influencing me in a way I do not like or that threatens to do so in the foreseeable future. If I ask what to do about that condition, I am asking how I can best influence that environment. In either case, we are dealing with flows of influence.

This viewpoint is closely related to the Taoist notion of yin and yang. If I seek to influence a situation, I am trying to act in a yang capacity, and to make the world yin to my intention. Conversely, if I see myself as the effect of my environment, I am yin to that environment, and it is yang to me.

The yang aspect is normally described as active, intentional, creative, dynamic, etc., as well as light and strong—the adjectives used in the I Ching. The yin aspect is identified with receptivity and acceptiv-

27

ity, as well as dark and weak—again the adjectives of the I Ching. In later Taoism, and some popular versions, the yin aspect is seen as bad or even evil, but this is not true in the original Taoism. Indeed, it is an explicit part of the earlier teachings that badness (not evilness, for the early Taoists did not recognize evil!) is the result of inappropriateness—being yin when the situation calls for a yang response, or yang when the times call for a yin response. One who knows the Tao (the Way) flows with the time, and so can be either yin or yang as appropriate.

It is easy to say that yang is active and yin passive. This, however, is an oversimplification, particularly on the yin side. As the I Ching makes clear, the yin side is not passive like a lump of clay waiting to be molded. It is rather like the earth that nourishes the seed without being concerned with what the seed may become. It is the mother that nourishes the child within her womb without knowing the infant's sex or the child's future. It is not passivity, but it is non-goal-directed. It is, instead, responsive to the immediacy of the moment and to its necessities.

On the other hand, it is not yang to ride a merry-go-round, even though there may be much motion involved, even voluntary motion. Movement is not the criterion, purpose is more like it. Or, perhaps time-binding is a better characteristic. If I move without thought for the future, I am simply responding to the moment—a yin response. If I seek a goal, then the seeking is yang. If I act without a goal, but with a strong sense that what I do affects the future, then I am still acting in a yang mode.

When we speak of flows of influence, we imply time-binding and persistence, whether intentional or not. The source of a flow is, therefore, yang. The target of the flow is yin to the degree that it simply responds in the moment. If, on the other hand, the target seeks to modify the influence, bending it according to the target's desires, then the target is also acting in a yang mode.

It is also a part of the Taoist view that neither yin nor yang exists in pure form in the manifest world. Yang always contains some yin, and vice versa. Intention, for example, must be based on an awareness of the reality that is the target of the intention; otherwise the desire is only fantasy. Since awareness is a yin aspect, the yang state of intention must be grounded in a yin component if it is to be effective. Likewise the responsiveness of yin remains consistent with the past.

This implies an ongoingness that is a yang aspect, and the ground of the yin mode.

Carrying this thought further, we can recognize that all flows are always bidirectional. If there is a flow of influence in one direction, there is also one in the other, or the first flow must be ineffective. We call a situation yin or yang because one of the pair of opposing flows of influence is visible, the other hidden. If I intend to influence people, I must remain as aware as possible of their state and of their response to my efforts. I must allow myself to be influenced by them; it is the flow of influence from them to me that allows me to create a flow of influence from me to them.

Conversely, if I want to understand a situation (a yin state), I must give it my attention—an intentional act directed towards the future, and therefore a yang mode. It is the flow of influence from me to it that makes possible the flow from it to me. Again, the flows in both directions are linked.

A consequence of this bidirectionality is that the two terminals of a flow may see quite different flows as the important ones. If you and I argue about what to do about something, we each express intentionality, seeing our own roles as both yang. Yet, if we are seriously seeking agreement—not simply debating—we each must listen to the other, and so be yin to the other. So the fact that, at one terminal, we see the state as primarily yang (or yin) does not prevent the other terminal from seeing its state as in the same condition. Neither does that perception describe the whole of what is going on.

This idea of bilateral flows is important to the I Ching. Indeed, its answers often focus attention on the hidden flows—the counterflows that we tend to ignore in our concentration on the flows we think are the problem. It is perhaps generally true that problems usually become more tractable when we give attention to the hidden flows. It may be that problems persist primarily because we usually notice only half the flows, and that, by looking for the hidden flows, we find a wholly new, and more complete, perspective.

The I Ching classifies situations according to the flows that are of principal importance. By identifying these flows, particularly those that we otherwise might ignore, the hexagrams give us a new and potentially powerful description of the reality around us. It is this that offers us a new view on our problems and so, ultimately, ourselves. It is this that accounts in part for the power of the book.

## STRUCTURE OF THE HEXAGRAMS

We are now ready to begin to consider the symbology of the I Ching and the source of the interpretations given to the hexagrams.

There are at least three traditional methods of decomposing the hexagrams. A hexagram can be seen as the combination of two trigrams or triplets of lines, three diagrams or pairs of lines, or six individual lines. In our work, we will pay principal attention to the first viewpoint, seeing a hexagram as composed of two trigrams.

Actually, the analysis goes further—each hexagram is seen as composed of four interlocking trigrams:

1. The INNER TRIGRAM: lines 1, 2, and 3 (the bottom three lines of a hexagram)

2. The OUTER TRIGRAM: lines 4, 5, and 6 (the top three lines)

3. The INNER NUCLEAR TRIGRAM: lines 2, 3, and 4 (near the bottom but excluding the bottom line)

4. The OUTER NUCLEAR TRIGRAM: lines 3, 4, and 5 (near the top but excluding the top line)

Of these four trigrams, the inner and outer are the primary ones; the nuclear trigrams may regarded as giving rise to, or lying behind, the inner and outer ones.

Consider first the inner and outer trigrams. The significances of these trigrams depend to an extent on the type of question being asked. What might be considered the most basic class of questions are those that ask "What should I do about such-and-such a situation?" Such a question immediately implies that there are two distinct parts to the problem: first, myself as the one that has the problem and the desire to do something about it; second, the situation I want to do something about. In other words, there is the actor and there is that which will be affected by the action.

Other types of questions also involve two components—otherwise there would be no problem. This is true even of the most abstract questions such as "What is the meaning of evil in the world?" Such a question implies myself as trying to understand and the world I see before me. There is, again, the actor and the environment, though the only action is to seek understanding.

In general, the inner trigram concerns the actor, or the one that has the problem that is worrisome. The outer trigram concerns the environment that poses the problem.

These statements should not be taken to imply that action is always needed, or desirable. It is difficult to avoid the implication of action in the English language, but we must be careful. What I should "do" about the situation may be to survive, waiting patiently for things to change. Maybe I should be a little more active, study the situation seeking to understand it better, or find a more favorable time for action. The I Ching accepts all these possibilities and others; the inner trigram can be either yin or yang. In the broad category of the question type, the inner trigram concerns how the questioner should respond to the situation he or she sees as a problem.

Similarly, the I Ching does not regard the environment as necessarily passive, blindly responsive to whatever action the questioner may take. The environment may be people with their own intentions, active participants in the events that pose the problem. Even an impersonal environment may impose severe limits on what can be done. If so, then it has a strong influence on the actor, and so may have a yang character. The environment, in fact, always influences to some degree what can be done. If this influence is seen as dominating, this is represented by the outer trigram being a yang one.

While the main interactions are described by the inner and outer trigrams, the conditions that create these aspects are identified by the inner and outer nuclear trigrams. What is it that makes the situation a problem for me? Why do I want to do anything about it? The answers to these questions are not obvious—often much less obvious than they first appear. Even such a simple and apparently straightforward thing as jumping out of the way of a truck can be questioned. Why do I consider it bad to get run over? A computer, for example, might not pay any attention to the possibility or recognize the truck as at all threatening. The inner nuclear trigram speaks of why the actor sees the situation as a problem.

The outer nuclear trigram is similarly related to the environment. What is it about the general environment that creates the problem? Being run over by a truck, for example, would be no problem if the truck did not have weight and inertia. This is a general feature of the physical world that makes the particular situation threatening. The outer nuclear trigram identifies those aspects that are relevant.

# ARRANGEMENT OF THE TRIGRAMS

There are several quite conventional ways to arrange the tri-grams. The one we have found most useful is the so-called *family arrangement*. This starts by classifying the eight possible trigrams as yin and yang, four of each type. Of the four yang trigrams, one is called the Father, the remaining three sons. Similarly, one yin trigram is called the Mother, the other three daughters. The three sons and the three daughters are arranged in order: the first born or eldest, the second born, and the last born or youngest. Table 2 shows the family arrangement, together with the translated names of the trigrams.

The designation of male and female—particularly when the female trigrams are called *weak* or *dark*—will offend many modern people. It is traditional; no doubt the early Chinese culture was strongly biased in ways that we now call sexist. However, it is worth emphasizing that the classification does not seem to have been intended as pejorative; the importance of the female side is fully rec-ognized in the I Ching. The female, or yin, aspects are those in which the flows are inward-directed, allowing the individual to receive infor-mation and influence from the world. They symbolize the cognitive, integrative, and supportive aspects of life. The masculine, or yang, aspects are those with outward-directed flows through which the individual seeks to affect the world. They include intention, decision, and action in various modes as discussed later.

In any case, we are talking here about symbols for deep arche-typal aspects. While the original metaphors were, no doubt, taken from the cultural norms of the day, they are now only convenient labels.

As discussed before, a solid line is yang, a broken one yin. The parents, then, are those trigrams in which each line has the character of the whole—the Creative, the Father, is composed only of yang lines; the Receptive, or Mother, has only yin lines.

In the other trigrams, two lines that have a common character may be understood to cancel each other. Thus, any trigram with two yin lines and one yang one is a yang trigram. This is perhaps sensible since intention, the yang aspect, will tend to hide the cognitive, inte-grative, and supportive aspects that may also be involved. On the opposite side, a trigram with two yang lines and one yin line is yin. In this case, we might view the two yang aspects as tending to pull in

**Table 2**

| THE FAMILY ARRANGEMENT | |
|---|---|
| **THE FATHER** | **THE MOTHER** |
| CH'IEN<br>The Creative | K'UN<br>The Receptive |
| **ELDEST SON** | **ELDEST DAUGHTER** |
| KÊN<br>Keeping Still, The Mountain | TUI<br>The Joyous, The Lake |
| **MIDDLE SON** | **MIDDLE DAUGHTER** |
| K'AN<br>The Abyss | LI<br>The Fire |
| **YOUNGEST SON** | **YOUNGEST DAUGHTER** |
| CHÊN<br>The Arousal, Thunder | SUN<br>The Wood, The Gentle |

opposite directions, immobilizing each other and allowing the yin aspect to become evident.

The family arrangement gives an important clue to the significance of the individual trigrams. Consider, first, the yang side. We
start with the Father, the Creative. While pure yang (or yin) cannot
exist in the manifest world, the Creative symbolizes a state that is as
nearly pure yang as is possible. It may be said to symbolize intention
or action itself. Coming to the sons, we are concerned with classifying
purpose and action. The broad intent of any action is to influence a
situation or people. More particularly, we can classify intention into
three categories: the origination of something new, the intention to
cope with something that already exists (altering or preserving it), the
completion or termination of something that has existed. The
sequence of these three aspects of action or intention is clear: first we
originate, next we cope, then we finish. This sequence is reflected in
the order of the sons, the Arousal, the Abyss, the Mountain.

On the yin side, the same kind of logic applies. The Mother, the
Receptive, symbolizes the state that is as nearly pure yin as is possible.
Therefore it symbolizes acceptance and awareness itself.

Coming to the daughters, acceptance and awareness are
attributes that are concerned with allowing influence to be felt. These
attributes can, again be classified into three types: acceptance of participation, awareness of the nature of the situation and of its details
and structure, and acceptance of the situation as something that has
its own reality, independent of my desires or concerns. This sequence
is reflected in the order of the daughters, the Wood, the Fire, and the
Joyous.

We will consider the significances of the trigrams in more detail
later and how their interpretations change according to the position
of the trigram. The very truncated meanings listed above are meant
only as a preliminary indication of what is involved.


# THE NATURE OF CHANGE

We have described the mechanism of casting the oracle, indicating that the lines may be found to be changing. The logic behind the
process is relatively clear, being founded on the well-known Taoist
principle that, whenever anything reaches its limit, it is likely to turn
into its opposite. A line is changing when it was obtained by a throw

of three heads or three tails. If the line is yang, all three coins showed the yang face. If the line is yin, all three showed the yin face. Since all the coins are the same, the throw is as yang or as yin as possible. Therefore, the principle says, the condition is about to turn into its opposite. A yang condition is about to become yin; a yin condition is about to become yang.

It is of interest to compare this with what we might consider the normal process, based on our usual causal-type thinking. We tend to expect that, when things reach their limit, they will simply back off. This can be described as a kind of principle of gradualism. It applies very well to many aspects of the physical world when they are viewed in the causal or linear mode. It may be said, in fact, to be a qualitative statement of linearity.

On the other hand, we are beginning to realize, even in scientific thought, that there are nonlinear domains, some of which are of overwhelming importance. Catastrophe theory, for example, is concerned with bistable, or multistable, situations in which a small influence can trigger huge effects, quite out of scale with the influences. Or, again, one of the recent technological developments having the most profound consequences has been the development of digital processes and the computer. The very foundation of such a machine is its use of bistability, again a violation of the principle of linearity.

It can be argued that, where linearity applies, we are concerned with quantitative effects. While these can be important, they are rarely catastrophic. Even when they lead to such disasters as famines, the effect is not catastrophic since the effect develops gradually. This gradualism allows us to know what we must do to alleviate the problem. If we fail to take the necessary steps, the results can of course be catastrophic, but that is a failure to take advantage of the linear nature of the problem, not a consequence of the linearity.

The process of using the linearity to avoid catastrophe is symbolized by the Abyss. The need to understand the linear nature of the problem is, in turn, symbolized by the Fire. (Fire in the I Ching is the light-giver, not the destroying conflagration.)

It can be further argued that true catastrophes occur where a bistable situation turns abruptly into its opposite as a result of an apparently trivial influence (or a multistable one into some other state). Such an event is symbolized by the Arousal (the unexpected or the novel), its effect by the Mountain (completion or destruction!), its impact by the Wood (participation), and the final consequences by the Joyous (acceptance of the final reality, whether cause for joy or not—perhaps "Serenity" would be a better name than the "Joyous").

This suggests, therefore, that the Taoist principle applies to the truly important things of life. It suggests also that the modern scientific principle of linearity is only useful in areas of lesser importance—areas in which substantial advances may be possible, but not those areas that represent real danger to the individual, to communities, to life itself.

# INTERPRETATION OF THE CHANGING LINES

In the original text, there is material associated with the individual lines, used when those lines are changing.[5] We can ask how the material on the lines can be developed.

As indicated, a line is changing when it has reached its limit and so is about to change into its opposite. Therefore, if the lines represent aspects of the whole situation (the viewpoint that sees the hexagram as composed of six single lines), the changing lines indicate those aspects that are relatively unstable. They may change spontaneously; they are also aspects that are most easily affected by what the actor does. A reading of the Duke of Chou's texts on the lines quickly shows that they may either focus attention on what should be done, or on what needs to be guarded against. They either point out opportunities or threats.

In interpreting the lines, it is also both reasonable and useful to look to see what hexagram results when each line is changed by itself. In the example we used before, shown in Figure 2, we had Difficulty at the Beginning with the 5th and 6th lines changing. The secondary hexagram, then, is #27, Corners of the Mouth. If we change simply the fifth line, we get #24, Return. The significance of the 5th line

---

5. We normally read only the material associated with those lines of the primary hexagram that are changing. An exception is when the text associated with the primary hexagram itself is too obscure. Scanning the material on all the lines may then help one interpret King Wen's material.

changing, therefore, can be approached by comparing the significance of Difficulty at the Beginning with that of Return. Similarly, if
we change only the 6th line, we get #42, Increase. We can discover
some of the significance of the 6th line by comparing the texts on Difficulty at the Beginning and Increase.

If there are more than two changing lines, we could carry the
process further and consider what hexagram is the result when we
change any subset of the set of changing lines. This gets somewhat
tedious, however, and may be pushing the logic too far. In any event,
the opportunity is somewhat rare—as has been indicated, there will
be more than two lines changing only about one time in six.

# THE PRIMARY AND SECONDARY
# HEXAGRAMS

Finally, we must consider the relation between the primary and
secondary hexagrams. The primary one, before changing any lines, is
clearly the most immediate answer to a question. The secondary one
is the result of changing all the changing lines. Therefore, its significance lies in its indication of what will happen if all the unstable
aspects change. It represents the greatest change in the situation that
is likely to occur, either spontaneously or as a result of the questioner's efforts.

This implies some time scale. It would be folly to assert any
limit on what can happen over an indefinite time period. On the other
hand, the question is also time-limited, whether the questioner
intends it or not. If I ask what I should do about something, I am not
asking for an answer in the indefinite future. I am probably only
thinking about what I might do during the next few hours or days or
weeks. Beyond that period, whatever it is, my question will have
become meaningless or irrelevant.

In fact, all questions of action or decision have an implied time
scale, whether we realize it or not. We do not need to be consciously
concerned with this time-scale in our question, however. When the
appropriate period has passed, the question will be recognized as
ancient history, and so will its answer. Therefore, if the throw of the

coins warns of threats or points out opportunities, we pay attention to them while our problem remains, and forget about them afterward.

This speaks of action questions. There are also questions of understanding and philosophy, where we are concerned with finding new insights for their own sake, not to guide decisions. The primary hexagram is, again, the most immediate answer to our question. In this case, however, the secondary hexagram tends to be a more global sort of answer, or one viewing the problem from a wider perspective.

This is reasonable. If the changing lines represent unstable aspects, then in a question that does not involve the process of time (i.e., that does not concern a decision or action) the named aspects will be ones that can be easily seen as their opposite, viewed from some different perspective. They do not so much speak of threats and opportunities as of sources of confusion.

To illustrate, if I should ask about the significance of some medical condition, the most immediate answer would presumably concern the pathology itself. The secondary hexagram might address the question in terms of the person's life style or general environment. It might even suggest the importance of an underlying karmic problem, perhaps speaking of the difficulty of trying to alleviate the physical condition while the karmic problem remains.

The example given above is just that—an example. I have not pursued such questions to any depth since I am not a medical person and it would be idle curiosity for me to pursue such questions. However, a probe into these areas would be quite in order for someone in the health field. I have, in fact, tried to help health practitioners interpret medical questions they have originated.

There are, then, various ways the secondary hexagram can be related to the primary one. It depends on the nature of the question, and on the state of mind of the questioner. During an actual session with the I Ching, finding the most appropriate viewpoint depends on intuition. The relation between the primary and secondary hexagrams, and the hexagrams and the changing lines, is properly a part of the second aspect of *Ling* described before—i.e., intuiting the relationship of the answer to the question.

# CHAPTER IV

# THE SOURCE OF ORACULAR INFORMATION

An inevitable question is the source of the information developed from a throw of the coins. Where does the answer to a question come from?

As stated in the Introduction, the Chinese have a word, *ling*, that names the ability to use the I Ching. It was stated, also, that *ling* has two components—the ability to use the coins or other techniques to obtain an answer, and the ability to see what that answer has to do with the question.

Regarding the first aspect, there is little we can say. As mentioned in Chapter II, Carl Jung found in the I Ching a direct application of his notion of synchronicity, the idea that the whole is connected in some mysterious way so that apparently disconnected events are still able to influence each other. This is clearly true—the question and the oracle exist in the same universe at the same time—but this says little about the nature of the connection. What is worse, it provides no scientifically acceptable hint of a process that might account for the I Ching. On a more esoteric level, there is the view that sees the physical world as controlled, maybe created, by Mind at some higher level of consciousness—a point of view that is not totally alien to some implications of modern physics, and to the ideas of some modern physicists. At a further reach, there are those who believe that the physical world is all illusion. These viewpoints can, perhaps, make it plausible to understand the I Ching as a vehicle connecting the different aspects of the manifest world. However, such views do not help much since they seem to offer little that might be useful, either for developing a student's *ling* or for extending the power of *ling* into other activities.

Of more interest is the second aspect of *ling*—the ability to see what the answer has to do with the question. This clearly involves intuition—what is the source of intuition? Where does the reader get the information used to interpret the I Ching's answer?

In this chapter, we will offer a tentative and partial answer. Whether this helps anyone or not is up to you. You are certainly free to reject it in whole or in part if you wish. Further, in labeling the viewpoint as tentative and partial, I am being entirely intentional. I fully expect that my own viewpoint will change with time—I hope it will evolve constructively. Further, there are grounds for believing that nobody (with the exception of any Bodhisatvas that may be around) can have a fully accurate and detailed understanding of the truth at the levels that must be considered here. At least, that conclusion must be essentially true if the general viewpoint has any validity. We return to this statement later.

We start with the idea of incorporeal spiritual entities.[6] We suppose that these entities are in perfect communication—through telepathy if you like, or simply because that is their nature.

Question: Given two entities in perfect communication, in what sense are they distinct? Can we really say that they are separate?

Answer: Probably not! At least there is no apparent sense in which they have separate identities in their own views of themselves. If A and B are in perfect communication, A cannot know whether a thought is its own or B's, or whether it is perceiving something itself or through B. It cannot know if it is making a decision or merely reflecting B's choice. It cannot even know if it is doing anything or is merely being aware of B's actions.

It seems clear, then, that, under the assumed conditions, no part of the whole can develop any useful and usable notion of selfhood or responsibility.

---

6. We avoid the use of the term "soul" since that word carries with it a number of considerations from the Judeo-Christian tradition that we do not want to assume.

This view is related to the statement in some esoteric traditions that humans are angels who have fallen in order to learn creativity and responsibility. The statement is made that angels are perfectly attuned to God's Will and so can only be agents of that Will, without creativity or initiative, automatons that can only obey His commands. The argument continues that the only way angels can learn selfhood, and develop the power of decision, is by separating from God, losing attunement with Him, and so experiencing alienation and error. Only then can they become self-knowing individuals with responsibility and the power of separation. The purpose of the Fall was to achieve these dimensions of being.

The view we prefer starts with the assumption of a vast sea of consciousness in which there is no distinction between self and not-self and no concept of individuation.

We suppose, next, that the idea of individuation arises within this sea. Seeking the experience of it, the first step might be the development of "nodes" within the sea. A node is a sort of concentration of awareness, perhaps focused on some particular part of the total awareness. If we assume that the physical universe already exists as a separate whole, we might suppose that each node focuses on a particular part of that universe. Perhaps the highest-level nodes might each focus on a particular cluster of galaxies within the universe.

Within a node, subnodes might then develop, focusing on successively smaller regions of the physical universe—first galaxies, then star clusters, then stars, then planets.

A further decomposition into subnodes could then arise focusing on particular aspects of the local region. The Earth node might first differentiate into life and other nodes, and the life node differentiate into different kinds of life down to the species level. At this level, we might expect a node that focuses on mankind as a whole.

Carrying the thought further, we can imagine that the node for mankind forms subnodes concerned, perhaps, with different peoples, defined by race, culture, nationality, whatever. These subnodes would then further specialize to groups of people, down to the over-soul of Seth, or to a subnode corresponding to what Vonnegut calls a "karass."

At some level, we reach the lowest level of nodes in the hierarchy. If you believe in linear reincarnation, this level names the spiritual entity that passes through successive incarnations until it is "freed from the wheel of life and death." Personally, I am more inclined to think that this lowest level is more of a group phenomenon—the node may have several or many incarnations going on at one time. This viewpoint actually merges the Judeo-Christian view with that of reincarnation. The individual incarnations are not repetitive. The part of the node that is incarnated in a single body returns to the node when that life is through, not to be reborn, but instead to be merged back into its source.

I do not claim that this description of the hierarchy is exact. As suggested, I hold no particular conviction on the separate reality of the physical universe. It may be that it is, in fact, created by some node at some level below the primal sea of spiritual awareness. If so, the division of attention and awareness among the nodes must be quite different from that sketched out here. The important thing is not the detailed nature of the hierarchy, but that the primal sea is decomposed into a hierarchical system of spiritual nodes.

At the lowest level, whatever it is, there is a focusing of aware-ness and attention, and so some approximation to a distinction between self and not-self. Yet the distinction remains blurred. Pre-sumably, there remains the potential for perfect communication, inherited from the primal sea. The communication is limited only to the extent that one node ignores what is received, or can receive, from another. The boundaries between the nodes remain fuzzy, blurred and shifting as attention shifts.

If the goal is to experience individuation—selfhood, the power of decision and action, the threat or promise of error, and responsibil-ity—something more is needed. This something is provided by incar-nation. It is added by the act of accepting a body with its sharp boundaries, and by the acceptance of the notion that the body is important. The latter is illusion. The node that accepts the body is invulnerable to anything that threatens the body, and the death of the body merely means that the experiences of the life that is ended are returned to the node. Yet the acceptance of that illusion and the belief that life is important are vital for the experience the node seeks—the experience of selfhood and of individuation.

The notion of karma fits into this schema. The node, presum-ably, seeks not only the illusion of self but to learn the responsibility that makes selfhood meaningful. Therefore, it uses its successive, and perhaps concurrent, incarnations to explore various problems of selfhood that lead to the awareness of responsibility.[7] An incarnation may fail badly, leading to the conclusion that a certain course of action or a certain set of viewpoints or considerations is wrong. It must then explore the consequences of other actions, other considerations. Perhaps the node accepts the need to be the target of the action that seems so wrong as a way to reach a full understanding of its wrongness. In any case, the logic of the node's purpose can easily lead to the events of one incarnation shaping the goal of another—a relationship between lives that is the Law of Karma.

All of this is preliminary to the question that concerns us—what is the source of intuition, or of what is called "channelled" information? If you accept the general viewpoint (however you may argue with its details), the answer becomes obvious. Awareness of things beyond the reach of a single person (defined by one's bodily identity) can only come via the hierarchy! He or she has been able, by some means, to obtain information from or through the higher-level nodes of the spiritual hierarchy.

The next question that follows from this answer is why that source of information is limited. Why don't we have full information on any subject we desire? Why can't we all "consult the Akashic records"?

As stated at the beginning, the viewpoint implies that no incarnate being can have full or exact knowledge of the reality contained in the spiritual nodes—with the possible exception of a Bodhisattva. The latter is, in Buddhistic thought and belief, an individual who stands on the threshold of full Buddhahood, but who turns back in order to help mankind. In our terms, a Bodhisattva is a person who has achieved all the goals of the spiritual node, and who therefore has developed a full awareness and understanding of all the implications of selfhood and individuation. The spiritual node that is incarnate in a Bodhisattva, therefore, has no further need for incarnation. However, he or she looks beyond the fuzzy limits of that node and accepts the goals of a higher node—perhaps the node of all mankind. The spirit returns to incarnation as a direct expression of the purpose of that higher node.

---

7. Is is important to realize what "responsibility" means. It is not guilt! It is, literally, the ability to respond, or to promise back. Guilt is, in fact, the last refuge of those who would avoid responsibility. Responsibility is a willingness to learn from the moment and to become and grow according to the lessons of the moment.

For most of us, incarnation is a device that serves the needs and goals of the immediate node. We have already observed that those goals require the illusion of the body's importance. They are likely also to require the suppression of other information. For example, it is likely to be necessary to suppress all but the most general information about a person's karmic purpose in this immediate life. If he or she knew, with a gut-level knowingness, what must be done in a given life, the knowingness would probably prevent doing it. As a simple, and simplistic, example, suppose the karmic purpose was to explore the feeling of being killed. If this was known, not on an intellectual level, but with the deep knowingness that can color a life, death would probably not have the impact the spiritual node intended to explore.

It follows, then, that a life is a game. It is a set piece that is intended to explore some particular type or types of situations and encounters, and to generate certain types of experience. The experience that is sought depends on our acting in ignorance of that purpose. Therefore, we must be isolated from certain information that is freely available to the spiritual node that has set up the game. We must act in ignorance, or our spiritual purpose would not and could not be served.

It does not follow that all higher-level information must be blocked. Indeed, this is clearly not the case—at least if you accept the evidence for past lives. However, there are reasons why access to much of the information is at least difficult. First, the blocks set up by the spiritual node may easily overstep the actual need. Second, it may be necessary in some lives to suppress awareness of the very existence of the spiritual node. This would not preclude intellectual awareness of the possibility, though it probably would mean an adamant disbelief. It would preclude any personal experiential evidence of the node's existence, and so would probably cause a relatively complete blocking of the intuitive channels from conscious awareness.

Finally, there is the phenomenon of cultural suppression. The different quality to information received through intuition (or other psychic channels) tends to create a general disbelief and invalidation, at least in our culture. This last factor has little to do with the spiritual hierarchy itself (except as that hierarchy is using the existing cultural environment), but can be an important element in limiting use of the channels.

If this viewpoint is accepted, even provisionally and with reservation, the I Ching (like other related devices such as the Tarot and runes) can be seen as a device that may facilitate bypassing some of the obstacles. Presumably, it would not permit bypassing those blocks that are actually dictated by the spiritual node, but it might help get closer to the blocked information than can easily be done otherwise. As for those who must deny all nonphysical phenomena, they will probably not consider the I Ching anyway, but will dismiss it as "nothing but superstitious nonsense." However, its use will provide distance between them and those who are open to the idea, and so may make it easier for the latter to attune themselves to the higher source. Similarly, the use of a device such as the I Ching will put distance between the practitioner and the cultural bias that denies the possibility of its utility.

If the ideas developed here have any validity, it follows that the spiritual levels should be reachable without any intermediary such as the I Ching. As a personal statement, I firmly believe this to be true. I also believe that the I Ching provides a very useful training toward that ability. The issue is, again, one of responsibility—of being willing and able to respond to the intuitive channels of knowledge and information without the need for an intermediary.

So the final conclusion is that we are dealing with a mystery, but one that is not entirely inaccessible or unintelligible. Furthermore, the mystery is one that is close to the heart of all spiritual development, being directly concerned with the relation of carnate man and woman to the higher levels that are of the spirit.

# CHAPTER V

# THE PRIMARY DUALITY: PRIEST AND SHAMAN

In Chapter III, the underlying world view of the I Ching was discussed briefly in terms of the yin-yang aspects of flows of influence. What was said there is quite general and seems entirely consonant with the traditional view of the I Ching. In this chapter, we consider a variation on this point of view that is the basis of the interpretation offered in this book. We call this view that of the duality between the shaman and priest, or the adept and the master. These labels are used to provide perspective, and to represent opposite roles that each of us play at different times. The duality is a general one applying to all levels of existence independent of titles, position, age, or sex. In particular, it is the duality between a person as a self-sufficient individual and as a participant in some larger whole.

As an individual, a person sees himself or herself as separate. We speak of "I" and think we know what this means. We claim to make decisions and exercise free will. In our more self-satisfied moments, we claim responsibility for what we do. Yet humans are also social beings, shaped and controlled in part by parents, peers, and culture in general. To what extent we really have free will, and whether we are more often controlled by our history, environment, and some habitual patterns of stimuli-response can be debated. As we move toward enlightenment, we generally come to acknowledge that we are part of some higher oneness we may call God, the Buddha, the Atman, the All, whatever. In our acceptance of this role, we acknowledge that much of what we do is not our own decision or evidence of any ultimate and limitless free will. Yet few would deny that we are responsible for much of what we do or fail to do. If nothing else, we acknowledge responsibility for our own state of enlightenment or lack thereof.

Humans are in fact both *individuals* with full responsibility for self and *participants* subservient to a unity we cannot ever fully grasp. At the highest level, Judeo-Christian teachings call that unity God. But long before we ever reach that level (if we ever do!), we are born into our culture and largely shaped by it. While we remain within that culture, we cannot ever fully know it. If, or when, we begin to have a perspective on its wholeness and to free ourselves of its limitations and strictures, we have begun to stand apart from it. Yet that merely means that our orientation has begun to shift to some higher-level whole in which we are now beginning to participate. We are then faced with a new mystery, a new unknown. We are not thereby freed from the mystery of participation.

The shaman, or adept, seeks to command the world. Being primarily concerned with the inner powers of self, he or she seeks to exercise the yang aspect that is influence. How successful this effort may be is of course another question. However, to have any hope of success, the would-be shaman must remain in touch with the world that is the target of the attempt. In addition, the shaman acts within the community or tribe and needs its validation. Therefore the shaman not only acts within the community, he or she also receives from it. Opposing flows coexist, and the shaman's acts are shaped in part by the community. Nevertheless, it is characteristic of the shaman that primary attention is on the responsibility of his or her self.

The priest, or master, seeks to be the vehicle through which some higher unity is manifested, the medium through which that unity's values are made manifest in the world and the community. The focus is on the source which is often assumed to be ineffable, ultimately unattainable, and unknowable. A priest may seek to influence others by example and self-discipline acting as the good shepherd. Or the effort may depend on force, intimidation, or worse, as during the

Inquisition or in modern oppressive dictatorships. The priest, therefore, can be a powerful initiator of action and so exercise what seems
to others an extreme yang principle. Yet the priest's true focus
remains on what he or she conceives as the source and on his or her
duty toward that source. In the priest's self-image, then, the vision is
of himself or herself as yin to that source.

These roles are not limited to those who claim the actual titles.
The priest's role is not limited to the religious life. The shaman's is
not confined to those who claim exceptional powers such as the wiz-
ards of popular conception or the spiritual warrior as described by
Castenada. We are each of us shamans when we see ourselves as
unique and self-sufficient and as acting out of our own insights and
intentions. We are each of us priests when we see our lives and actions
as controlled by some external source, be it God, the gods, humanity,
society, government, fate, luck, physical limitation, whatever. The
source can be anything deemed worthy of allegiance. The emphasis of
the priest is on interpreting the source, whatever it is, not on being
the source. The shaman may claim to deal with divine powers or to
manipulate external forces. The claim, however, is that these powers
or forces can be commanded or persuaded to serve the shaman's purpose. Consider, for example, a scientist in the laboratory. Seeking to
wrest understanding from nature, he or she acts as a shaman. On the
other hand, when the scientist/shaman claims a position in the establishment of his or her profession and invokes the authority of that
establishment, the shaman becomes the priest. Then the shaman has
been transmuted into the priest.

Similarly, the priest may claim incontestable authority known
only to the elect. He or she may claim a special knowledge of truth
and decry all who would dispute the doctrine as ignorant victims of
self-deception if not actually willfully sinful. This extremism has been
evident in many religions at many times, but it is not confined to the
religious arena. Indeed, it is all too common in many areas of life. The
priest, following the logic of his or her role, sees the greatest fault to
be a lack of commitment to the source. The greatest threat is the
doubt that weakens commitment. As a result, others may see the
priest as arrogant and intolerant, even monomaniacal. Hitler was
probably a priest in this sense when he spoke of manifest destiny. That
the priest must be humble before the claimed source does not suggest
that he or she must be humble before others! The priest remains a ser-

vant only of the source and, in the role's more extreme manifesta-
tions, acknowledges responsibility only to that source.

In our interactions with humanity, society, culture, our tribe,
our peers, whatever, we are both priests and shamans. In the shaman's
role, we claim rights and powers as individuals and, at least to some
degree, acknowledge our responsibility for ourselves. In this we take
the shaman's role. Yet we also participate in the various communities
of our lives and accept, often without question, the teachings, cus-
toms and values of those communities. When we do, we take the
priest's role.

It is of course an oversimplification to see only the priestly and
shamanistic roles. In our culture we mix the two in ways that generally weaken both. We expect the community to support us and are apt
to feel bitter and betrayed when it does not. This contradicts the role
of the priest who is not permitted to question the virtue of whatever
the source does or fails to do. Neither does it fit the shaman's role
who ideally is independent of any community. In fact, the shaman, in
principle, should see any failure as a consequence of his or her own
ignorance or misunderstanding. The ideal shaman, therefore, like the
priest but for different reasons, has no basis for resenting any lack of
support. In a real sense, then, we are priests, but only to an ideal
source that is, at best, approximated by reality. Equally, we are shamans, but only until we are frustrated by our society, and find ourselves unable to exercise shamanistic powers as we think we should.
The resultant ambivalence may be useful as it tends to protect us col-
lectively from the excesses that are possible in the undiluted roles.
However, we can also see in the resultant confusion the seeds of many
of the problems of our society and age.

Those who explicitly claim the title of priest or shaman, or who
have other comparable titles, fill acknowledged offices. The rest of us
play similar roles without the title. We must, for life demands it of us.
A person without explicit authority or power must still live. If a person conceives the goal of action as arising out of an inner need or
desire, he or she acts in the shaman's role, no matter where blame is
placed if the act falls short of the goal. If the person sees the act as
responsive to the imperative of some external authority, the priest's
role is being played, no matter how bitter failure may seem. In all
actions, in all life, each of us is a blend of shaman and priest.

The paradox of free will versus determinism remains an illusion,
the consequence of the bidirectional quality of all flows in the world

of our experience. As priest, a person sees his or her own self as serving the values and goals of an external source. Yet, the acceptance of those values and goals and the willingness to be controlled by them is a more or less deliberate choice, an act of free will. The individual may ignore or deny this, claiming to have "been called" to serve God, or scientific truth, or the ways of our forefathers, or whatever. Yet there are many who have made different choices, demonstrating that the choice to serve the named source is an open one that depends on the individual. In making such a personal choice, the individual acts as a shaman. Likewise, the individual who takes the shaman's role in the name of free will asserts that he or she acts out of inner selfhood, and so is master of his or her own destiny. Yet whatever such a person does is done in the context of the physical and social realities of his or her world. The individual, therefore, is controlled in part by external elements. The shaman may deny this vigorously, yet it is in that context that he or she acts. This is true even of the choice to be independent. Therefore, in the individual's decision to take the path of the shaman and so to seek to discover and extend the self's freedom and power, he or she is in part taking the role of the priest. It cannot be otherwise. Neither the priest's nor the shaman's view of life is complete. The reality is always a blend of both. In each act as a shaman, there is an element of the priest's function, and vice versa.

Despite the illusory nature of the dichotomy of free will versus determinism, it remains highly significant. As a person sees his or her primary role, so does he or she respond to the lessons of experience. That response has much to do with how the person sees the path to learning and, hopefully, growth.

Ideally, the priest sees failure as evidence of unworthiness and consequent separation from the source. His or her response will therefore be one of guilt or shame, leading to atonement. Pride becomes a deadly sin precisely because it separates the person from the source, humility a virtue because it opens the person to the source. The path to growth is seen as through abasement to the ineffable source.

Ideally, again the shaman sees failure as an opportunity lost either through insufficient understanding or a lack of sufficient will. Failure can be seen as a reason for confusion or even despair, but never guilt. Pride becomes a virtue because it reinforces the commitment beyond all failure and discouragement, humility a sin because it weakens intention and the power of will. For a shaman, the path to growth is through study and effort, an exercise in will.

Despite these contrasts, the two roles interact in subtle ways. The shaman must act within the context of some community despite the claim, and perhaps the belief, that he or she acts only out of an inner vision. In fact, the shaman needs the community as an arena in which power can be used and its effects measured. It is only by this testing that he or she can come to know more fully his or her own beingness. In accepting the community as an arena for testing power, the shaman takes the role of the priest.

The priest, on the other hand, seeks to interpret and fulfill what the source requires. He or she seeks to serve and to make the source manifest through that service. Yet the priest's actions cannot help but be shaped by his or her own understanding of the source. Since the source is, by definition, ineffable and so ultimately unknowable, the priest must test his or her understanding and interpretation. Like the shaman, he or she must measure the value and power of action by its effects. The priest, therefore, takes the role of the shaman in seeking to become a better priest, the more perfect servant. In the end, the distinction between the two roles must be recognized as illusion.

Dualities, it is said, must be transcended. That is true, but it does not mean abandonment. It means, instead, reaching a state in which we are no longer trapped by the illusion of the duality, no longer bound to a fixed pattern of stimulus-response based on a limited view of the truth the duality represents. Priesthood and shamanism name different views of self, of the world of experience, and of how the two relate. To the extent we understand these differences we can begin to use both roles according to their strengths and as may be appropriate in any given situation. While acting in one role we can know the reality and values of the other, and understand what would make that other role appropriate. We can then learn and grow from each role as it becomes appropriate to the immediate situation.

The duality of the priest's and shaman's roles can be analyzed into a structure that encodes the various ways they interweave. This is precisely what we have endeavored to do. The result is the interpretation of the I Ching presented here.

# A NOTE ON SEXIST ECHOES

In the preceding material and what follows, we have referred to the priest and the shaman. To some, these words may sound sexist, particularly in the reference to the "priest." If so, we can only apologize while insisting that nothing of the sort is intended. The difficulty is that, in our culture, a "priestess" is not the same as a feminine priest. We do not have priestesses in the religions that have priests, or not many of them. The idea of a priestess, therefore, carries with it associations to either ancient cultures or minor religions or cults. The sense we wished to invoke with the label is generally associated with the word "priest," not "priestess." We therefore have felt it necessary to use the term "priest" without qualification.

The label "shaman" does not offer the same problem. Shamans are not widely known in our culture so that the word does not carry an automatic implication of either sex. Furthermore, shamans are often women, particularly among those who claim the title in our culture. In fact, the two practicing shamans the author knows are both women.

In any case, we do not mean to imply anything about the sex of any practitioner. Rather, the terms are meant to indicate where he or she looks for the source of knowledge and inspiration. Indeed, we have emphasized that we use those terms in a sense that transcends the cultural matrix of their common usage. They represent modes of thought and belief, not positions or knowledge or even belief itself, and certainly not any sexist belief or attitude.

It is worth acknowledging that the culture in which the I Ching arose was indeed sexist, albeit not entirely as that term is used today. Men and women were seen as having very definite and quite separate roles. There does not seem to have been any implication of suppression or contempt in this, merely a statement of what they saw as reality. Indeed, this is an instance of what became one of the major principles of Confucianism: That each person has a specific role to play in life, and that individual happiness and worth comes from recognizing and accepting one's proper role. Further, the foundations of society, and its stability, were seen as resting on people understanding and accepting this principle. The clearest statement of this principle in the I Ching is probably in the Confucian commentary on Chia Jên, The Family, 37. The Wilhelm/Baynes translation of this material is as follows:

> THE FAMILY. The correct place of the woman is
> within; the correct place of the man is without. That
> man and woman have their proper places is the greatest
> concept in nature.
>
> Among the members of the family there are strict rul-
> ers; these are the parents. When the father is in truth a
> father and the son a son, when the elder brother is an
> elder brother and the younger brother a younger
> brother, the husband a husband and the wife a wife,
> then the house is on the right way.
>
> When the house is set in order, the world is established
> in a firm course.

This passage is also a reference to the family arrangement of the
trigrams which are credited to King Wen. Since that arrangement
identifies half the trigrams as feminine, half as masculine, it also can be
seen as reflecting a sexist bias in the culture that existed even in King
Wen's time. Yet that arrangement does not denigrate one sex over the
other, it merely identifies them as different with different attributes.
We can only ask that modern man and woman look beyond this cultural echo to the underlying reality of the archetypes that are the real
content of the I Ching.

# CHAPTER VI

# THE TRIGRAMS:
# KEY WORDS
# AND PHRASES

In the last chapter, we discussed the duality that we labeled as that between the shaman and the priest. More generally, it is the duality between one as an individual and one as a member of a larger community.

In Chapter IV, we discussed one possibility for the source of information that may be the basis of all truly intuitive functions, including the I Ching. If the hypothesis identified there is reasonably near the truth, then it follows that humankind incarnates in order to experience and experiences in order that the spiritual entity may become.

Table 2 in Chapter III shows the so-called Family Arrangement of the trigrams attributed to King Wen. This arrangement identifies, in part, the generic meanings of the trigrams, independent of any context or their positions in the hexagram.

Also mentioned in Chapter III are the four significant positions a trigram can have in a hexagram. We discussed there the different contexts that are involved in these positions. Recapitulating what was said there, the four positions and their significances are as follows:

The INNER TRIGRAM, lines 1, 2, and 3.

The attitude and viewpoint of the questioner who confronts a problem—or how he or she should or might approach the question.

The INNER NUCLEAR TRIGRAM, lines 2, 3, and 4.

The inner source of the questioner's attitude or viewpoint. The deeper significance of his or her attitude and viewpoint.

The OUTER NUCLEAR TRIGRAM, lines 3, 4, and 5.

The aspect of the outer reality that has created the situation the questioner sees as a problem.

The OUTER TRIGRAM, lines 4, 5, and 6.

The condition in the external world that the questioner sees as a problem, and which he or she seeks to understand or influence.

These various viewpoints can now be developed into a consistent set of interpretations of the trigrams in the four positions. The details of this development are given in Chapter IX, The Trigrams. Here we summarize the results in Table 3, associating key words and phrases with the various trigrams in the four positions. For a more complete understanding of what is implied by these words and phrases, the reader should consult Chapter X. The material of Table 3, however, will be used in the next two chapters that deal with the hexagrams. There, for each hexagram, we describe the hexagram's structure in terms of the trigrams, and, for each trigram, repeat the associated word or phrase as given in Table 3.

## Table 3

| KEY WORDS FOR THE TRIGRAMS IN THE FOUR POSITIONS | | | |
|---|---|---|---|
| | **INNER** | **INNER NUCLEAR** | **OUTER** | **OUTER NUCLEAR** |
| **CH'IEN** | The Shaman | Intention to Experience | Imminence | Principle of Autonomy |
| **CHÊN** | Intention to Initiate | Intention to Experience Origination | Unpredict-ability | Principle of Uniqueness |
| **K'AN** | Intention to Control | Intention to Experience Control | Flux of Change | Principle of Change |
| **KÊN** | Intention to Terminate | Intention to Experience Finality | Finality | Principle of Finality |
| **K'UN** | The Priest | Principle of Reality | Suscepti-bility | Principle of Potentiation |
| **SUN** | Participation | Principle of Involvement | Integrity | Principle of Consistency |
| **LI** | Perception | Principle of Discrimination | Lawfulness | Principle of Lawfulness |
| **TUI** | Acceptance | Principle of Assimilation | Continuity | Principle of Comprehensi-bility |

# CHAPTER VI

# THE HEXAGRAMS: BOOK 1

As indicated, the sequence of the hexagrams is traditional and thought to date from king Wen. So too is the division into two books: Book 1 containing hexagrams 1 through 30 and Book 2 with hexagrams 31 through 64.

We may wonder what is the significance of this arrangement. We suggest that the sequence lists progressive steps on the path to enlightenment while the division into two books reflects two major themes on this path. In this view, the first theme starts with the existence and nature of duality in The Creative (#1) and The Receptive (#2). Subsequently, it describes how the disciple must address issues of the outer reality and his or her own place in the world. This process reaches a climax in Biting Through (#21) to be followed by a series of consolidation steps through The Fire (#30). In the second theme, the disciple must confront the ultimate nature of the inner reality. The climax here is in Coming To Meet (#44) which is again followed by a series of development and consolidation steps.

We have not emphasized this viewpoint here, but it has influenced the material. Therefore we have felt it appropriate to preserve both the order and the division.

# 1
# CH'IEN
# THE CREATIVE

STRUCTURE

Outer: The *Creative*: Imminence.
  Outer Nuclear: The *Creative*: The principle of autonomy.
  Inner Nuclear: The *Creative*: The intention to experience.
Inner: The *Creative*: The shaman.

COMMENTARY

The shaman seeks to impose his or her will upon the world—to create what is desired, to halt what is opposed, or to alter what is not according to the shaman's vision. Yet the world is what it is, not necessarily what the shaman would make of it. The shaman may succeed somewhat, but only by acting according to its reality.

The shaman's ultimate goal, however, is not to master the world. Rather, he or she has taken up the mantle of the shaman in order to experience and so to further understanding of self and the self's power and to seek the responsibility that is at the core of power.

Seeking self, the nature of will is tested in order to find the one who wills.

# 2
# K'UN
# THE RECEPTIVE

## STRUCTURE

Outer: The *Receptive*: Susceptibility.
  Outer Nuclear: The *Receptive*: The principle of potentiation.
  Inner Nuclear: The *Receptive*: The principle of reality.
Inner: The *Receptive*: The priest.

## COMMENTARY

The priest acknowledges the dominion in which he or she acts and has being. Accepting duty and the necessity for the sacrifice of self, the priest seeks alignment with the unknown and the unknowable, and to empty self in order to receive the ineffable.

The world is susceptible to the priest's presence. What the priest is has effect; the world is altered by his or her being. Out of the dark realm of potentiality the actuality of the present emerges and the quietness of the inner center is nurtured.

Knowing the responsibility of acceptance, the seeker finds the freedom of submission.

# 3

# CHUN

# DIFFICULTY
# AT THE
# BEGINNING

## STRUCTURE

Outer: The *Abyss*: The flux of change.
    Outer Nuclear: The *Mountain*: The principle of finality.
    Inner Nuclear: The *Receptive*: The principle of reality.
Inner: The *Arousal*: The intention to initiate.

## COMMENTARY

The shaman knows the pain of birth as what is willed is summoned from the womb of potentiality. What is born is unknown; what it will become cannot be known with certainty.

One who seeks the role of the shaman may claim the virtue of intention, fearing the truth of what is not bound to his or her command. Yet intention must be swamped by the flux of change and vision soon lost in the finality of time.

The seeker confronts the finality of change beyond all intention. The fact may be denied so that the seeker may hold intact belief in power. Or responsibility for the consequences may be denied, and only the intention acknowledged. Yet what is gained?

It is by the acceptance of uncertainty without denying responsibility that the seeker can begin to be the true shaman, and to seek what he or she may yet become.

# 4

# MÊNG

# YOUTHFUL FOLLY

## STRUCTURE

Outer: The *Receptive*: Finality.
Outer Nuclear: The *Receptive*: The principle of potentiation.
Inner Nuclear: The *Arousal*: The intention to experience origination.
Inner: The *Abyss*: The intention to control.

## COMMENTARY

The shaman, in ignorance, may seek to control reality. The world, however, will only enforce the error of that folly.

The future contains the potential for all things, the past is closed by time. What the shaman does cannot be corrected, nor can what is left undone be corrected. Error, therefore, cannot be repaired, yet also cannot be avoided since there must always be ignorance before the fullness of potential that is the world. It is only as the shaman uses the power, not to avoid error but to discover it and so seek to learn from it that there can be success.

The seeker, acknowledging the consequences of effort, influences the world but does not shape it. Rather, it is the self that is shaped. By the acceptance of unknowingness, the self is enabled to move toward that which seeks its own becoming.

# 5
# HSÜ
# WAITING

## STRUCTURE

Outer: The *Abyss*: The flux of change.
　　Outer Nuclear: The *Fire*: The principle of lawfulness.
　　Inner Nuclear: The *Joyous*: The principle of assimilation.
Inner: The *Creative*: The shaman.

## COMMENTARY

The shaman, acting within a world in continual flux, seeks experience. In the inability to anticipate the consequences of action, the shaman recognizes the need to act quietly lest action magnify the turbulence of becoming.

In the limits of perception and understanding, the world seems chaotic. Yet behind all appearance is the Law—the order that enforces all becoming. The appearance of chaos is itself expression of the Law, though the logic may be beyond all comprehension.

The shaman, contemplating the world with eyes unclouded by desire, can learn something of the Law though not its fullness.

# 6
# SUNG
# CONFLICT

## STRUCTURE

Outer: The *Creative*: Imminence.
  Outer Nuclear: The *Wood*: The principle of consistency.
  Inner Nuclear: The *Fire*: The principle of discrimination.
Inner: The *Abyss*: The intention to control.

## COMMENTARY

If the shaman seeks to control the environment, he or she must fail. Yet even in that failure, discrimination can be learned and its use. In failure can be found lessons of the things of the world, and what cannot be done with them.

The world is imminent. What the shaman does cannot be undone, what is not done cannot later be changed. In the process of the world's becoming, it remains forever in the harmony of its own self-consistency, forever beyond the seeker's power despite all intention or desire. Therefore, if the seeker looks beyond the act, he or she must know failure. Yet who is it that has failed?

In the willingness to acknowledge failure even while striving, the seeker finds the self that seeks.

# 7
# SHIH
# THE ARMY

## STRUCTURE

Outer: The *Receptive*: Susceptibility.
Outer Nuclear: The *Receptive*: The principle of potentiation.
Inner Nuclear: The *Arousal*: The intention to experience origination.
Inner: The *Abyss*: The intention to control.

## COMMENTARY

The shaman seeks to control the environment of his or her existence. The effort tests the nature of origination and desire. The world is affected by what the shaman does, responding according to its potentialities. Yet the mystery remains for the seeker cannot ever know in full what has been done.

In the contemplation of action and of being, the seeker can discover responsibility. Seeing what has been and contemplating the vision that gives purpose to action, something may be learned of the nature of power and its limits. Yet, to profit from the experience and truly move toward the power of the shaman, the seeker must acknowledge not only the vision but also the reality of the unintended consequences.

Confronting both success and failure and denying neither, the seeker becomes and, in the process, recreates the self.

# 8

# PI

# HOLDING TOGETHER (UNION)

## STRUCTURE

Outer: The *Abyss*: The flux of change.
Outer Nuclear: The *Mountain*: The principle of finality.
Inner Nuclear: The *Receptive*: The principle of reality.
Inner: The *Receptive*: The priest.

## COMMENTARY

The priest stands before the altar of the world, accepting its reality and seeking to attune self to the unknowable. Making the self empty, illusion is sacrificed so that the seeker may become the instrument of mystery.

The world is ever changing as events succeed each other without end. Time moves, and the past is dissipated in the mists of history. The priest, accepting the appearance of the world and acknowledging his or her own insufficiency, becomes the servant. In the ritual of sacrifice, the seeker bows before the inner mystery, the Void that is the center of beingness.

# 9

# HSIAO CH'U

# THE TAMING POWER OF THE SMALL

## STRUCTURE

Outer: The *Wood*: Integrity.
  Outer Nuclear: The *Fire*: The principle of lawfulness.
  Inner Nuclear: The *Joyous*: The principle of assimilation.
Inner: The *Creative*: The shaman.

## COMMENTARY

The shaman seeks to manifest the power of will. What is done has effect, yet the integrity of the world is unshaken; the world remains forever faithful to a deeper Law.

The shaman has power, but, to use that power, he or she must act according to the reality of the world. Yet there remains the power of choice and the seeker still bears responsibility for what is done or not done and for the consequences though they conform to the Law, not necessarily to the shaman's desire.

It is by acceptance of the Law that cannot be known in full and by recognition of the limits of what can be known that the shaman is enabled to test the nature of will.

# 10
# LÜ
# TREADING

## STRUCTURE

Outer: The *Creative*: Imminence.
   Outer Nuclear: The *Wood*: The principle of consistency.
   Inner Nuclear: The *Fire*: The principle of discrimination.
Inner: The *Joyous*: Acceptance.

## COMMENTARY

The world in which the seeker moves is imminent with an impact that cannot be denied. In order to learn, the seeker becomes the priest, accepting without challenge the world's reality and the lessons of its experience.

Contemplating the world, the seeker stands apart, creating distance and perspective and the illusion of separation. Naming self as unique, he or she claims an existence that suspends the truth of the self's participation in the whole. Yet, knowing this for illusion, the seeker remains free to comprehend the truth of experience.

Standing apart in order to discriminate, the priest accepts in order to become. In the duality of separation and experience, the seeker approaches the paradox of being. Then the seeker may discover the challenge of both discrimination and acceptance.

# 11
# T'AI
# PEACE

STRUCTURE

Outer: The *Receptive*: Susceptibility.
Outer Nuclear: The *Arousal*: The principle of uniqueness.
Inner Nuclear: The *Joyous*: The principle of assimilation.
Inner: The *Creative*: The shaman.

COMMENTARY

The shaman acts according to his or her will. The world responds, being susceptible to what is done. Out of the darkness of the Void, the new is manifested, a consequence of the shaman's power. Yet the act is meaningless unless the seeker also assimilates its consequences and accepts the lessons of experience.

Who can know the full consequences of any act? The world is influenced by what the shaman does, but the instant of doing is unique within the flow of time and the world remains unpredictable. The shaman's claim of power is therefore limited, for none can know the fullness of what has been done.

In the acknowledgment of imperfection and error, yet also in the recognition of responsibility, the shaman tests the nature of will and so learns to command self.

STRUCTURE

> Outer: The *Creative*: Imminence.
>> Outer Nuclear: The *Wood*: The principle of consistency.
>> Inner Nuclear: The *Mountain*: The intention to experience finality.
> Inner: The *Receptive*: The priest.

COMMENTARY

The priest knows the sacrifice of being in the experience of time as it seals the past.

The world to which the priest gives service is imminent with an impact that cannot be denied. It bears witness to a self-consistency that binds the processes of its becoming. Bowing before the unknown rulership that enforces the reality of experience, the priest can but accept what is given.

By service, the priest finds the limits of self. By the acceptance of sacrifice, he or she finds silence. Bowing before the altar of existence, the seeker acknowledges the fulfillment of the instant.

# 13

# T'UNG JÊN

# FELLOWSHIP WITH MEN

## STRUCTURE

Outer: The *Creative*: Imminence.
   Outer Nuclear: The *Creative*: The principle of autonomy.
   Inner Nuclear: The *Wood*: The principle of involvement.
Inner: The *Fire*: Perception.

## COMMENTARY

The priest stands apart from the environment in order to perceive. Yet the imminence of the world commands attention; its impact cannot be denied. In the autonomy of its becoming, the world enforces the seeker's experiencing, creating opportunity to learn.

The priest has chosen to be involved and to be subordinate to the world's reality in order to test the truth of that involvement. However, by standing apart in order to perceive, the seeker qualifies that participation and his or her priesthood, and so seeks to compromise the world's imminence. Yet there is no other path to understanding, no other way to contemplate the implications of experience.

In the paradox of participation and separation, the seeker has the opportunity to become.

# 14

# TA YU

# POSSESSION IN GREAT MEASURE

## STRUCTURE

Outer: The *Fire*: Lawfulness.
Outer Nuclear: The *Joyous*: The principle of comprehensibility.
Inner Nuclear: The *Creative*: The intention to experience.
Inner: The *Creative*: The shaman.

## COMMENTARY

The shaman, intending to experience, seeks to impose will on the environment. The world, however, is ever lawful; it responds to what is done, but only according to the Law.

The world is lawful, but the seeker cannot know the fullness of the Law while yet a part of the world and so subject to the Law. Yet, the Law can be understood to some degree according to the seeker's experience and perceptions. Therefore experience serves the self, and seeking can be rewarded.

The shaman must ultimately fail if he or she seeks to command the world. Success lies in the realization that the seeking is but a way to test knowledge and will.

# 15
# CH'IEN
# MODESTY

## STRUCTURE

> Outer: The *Receptive*: Susceptibility.
>> Outer Nuclear: The *Arousal*: The principle of uniqueness.
>> Inner Nuclear: The *Abyss*: The intention to experience control.
> Inner: The *Mountain*: The intention to terminate.

## COMMENTARY

The shaman intends to terminate what no longer serves. In this, he or she seeks to test the nature of control for the surest path to control is by the ending of what is no longer wanted.

The world is susceptible to what the shaman does as it manifests the principle of novelty. By terminating what has been, the shaman makes possible the new with minimum interference. What will emerge cannot be known in full, or what will be the entire consequence of what has been done. Therefore, the seeker acts only to end what is no longer appropriate, and does not seek to command the world.

Knowing the limits of power, the seeker remains aware and so accepts the role of shaman. By doing so, he or she also accepts the freedom of responsibility.

# 16
# YÜ
# ENTHUSIASM

STRUCTURE

Outer: The *Arousal*: Unpredictability.
Outer Nuclear: The *Abyss*: The principle of change.
Inner Nuclear: The *Mountain*: The intention to experience finality.
Inner: The *Receptive*: The priest.

COMMENTARY

The priest moves within a world that is ever unpredictable as it moves according to the principle of change. Not knowing what may happen or understanding the fullness of what can be seen, the priest can only acknowledge the flux of time and form while bowing before the unknown and unknowable.

Within, the priest recognizes the mystery of completion and of ending. How can what has been cease to be? How did the self that was become the self that is? How is death followed by birth?

In the arena of the world, the priest acknowledges the parable of inner drama and so furthers what must be.

# 17
# SUI
# FOLLOWING

STRUCTURE

Outer: The *Joyous*: Continuity.
Outer Nuclear: The *Wood*: The principle of consistency.
Inner Nuclear: The *Mountain*: The intention to experience finality.
Inner: The *Arousal*: The intention to initiate.

COMMENTARY

The shaman originates in order to experience closure. Closure is the result of origination since, in creation, there is always the ending of what might have been but no longer can be. The moment of action closes the reality of the past, it is by the new that the ending of the old is made manifest.

The world moves in continual becoming, yet remains self-consistent. The seeker moves within it, and what he or she does cannot be inconsistent with the reality of the world. The shaman may claim the power of decision and origination, yet cannot violate the harmony of the world's becoming. What he or she does, therefore, is part within that harmony. Its principal importance is not within the world, but in the self.

As actor within the world, the shaman is one with it. As one who contemplates the mystery of selfhood, and also who sees action as the tool of testing but not of mastery, the seeker looks for the inner harmony of self-knowledge.

# 18
# KU

# WORK ON WHAT HAS BEEN SPOILED

*Decay*

## STRUCTURE

Outer: The *Mountain*: Finality.
Outer Nuclear: The *Arousal*: The principle of novelty, uniqueness.
Inner Nuclear: The *Joyous*: The principle of assimilation.
Inner: The *Wood*: Participation.

## COMMENTARY

The priest is a participant in a reality that transcends all reach. By the self's participation, it becomes possible to assimilate the lessons of experience, and to see events within the framework of that participation.

The world of the seeker's experience is final, but the limits it imposes are conditional. Its present is determined by the past and so remains unalterable. Yet judgment can be changed and values altered. By acceptance of the finality of what has been, the seeker can allow the self to reexamine the significance of what has been and to reconsider what may be learned.

It is by acceptance that the seeker allows self the freedom of the future and the choice of becoming.

# 19

# LIN

# APPROACH

## STRUCTURE

Outer: The *Receptive*: Susceptibility.
Outer Nuclear: The *Receptive*: The principle of potentiation.
Inner Nuclear: The *Arousal*: The intention to experience origination.
Inner: The *Joyous*: Acceptance.

## COMMENTARY

The priest accepts experience, making it part of the self. By doing so, the intention to experience origination is fulfilled, for the act of creation is empty if the creator does not acknowledge what has been done.

The world is susceptible to the seeker's actions, being ruled by the principle of potentiation. By the act of origination, the seeker summons out of the Void what can be, giving it shape and substance. Yet the consequences may not be according to intention or expectation. There is no law that commands reality to the seeker's will. Failing in intent, the seeker must choose whether to accept or deny the truth of what has been done. It is the seeker's choice whether to learn or merely suffer.

# 20
# KUAN
# CONTEMPLATION

## STRUCTURE

Outer: The *Wood*: Integrity.
Outer Nuclear: The *Mountain*: The principle of finality.
Inner Nuclear: The *Receptive*: The principle of reality.
Inner: The *Receptive*: The priest.

## COMMENTARY

The priest prepares the way. The inward awareness of the unknowable pervades his or her being, making sacred the seeker's presence. On the priest is the duty of acceptance and the challenge of the unnameable.

The world has an integrity that cannot be violated. What happens must always be appropriate to what has been, the present remains a reflection of the past even as it completes it. The priest, standing in silent contemplation, remains receptive, empty, before the wholeness that he or she senses but cannot know.

Recognizing self as part within the wholeness, the seeker makes the self its symbol and its silent voice.

# 21

# SHIH HO

# BITING
# THROUGH

Outer: The *Fire*: Lawfulness.
Outer Nuclear: The *Abyss*: The principle of change.
Inner Nuclear: The *Mountain*: The intention to experience finality.
Inner: The *Arousal*: The intention to initiate.

## COMMENTARY

The seeker, taking the role of the shaman, intends to originate so as to experience finality and closure. The act is irrevocable; it cannot later be reshaped to make its consequences fit the intention.

The world is lawful; it ever changes but always according to its own reality. The seeker acts, and what is done is also lawful. How could it be otherwise? Yet the seeker cannot know the fullness of the Law, or the entire consequences of the act. Acknowledging the failure of intention through observing what has been done, the seeker can only learn. Yet the trial must be made for it is only in the effort that there is hope.

It is only in the failure of effort that the seeker can learn.

## STRUCTURE

Outer: The *Mountain*: Finality.
Outer Nuclear: The *Arousal*: The principle of uniqueness.
Inner Nuclear: The *Abyss*: The intention to experience control.
Inner: The *Fire*: Perception.

## COMMENTARY

The priest contemplates the world and its events, seeking to test the nature of process and its control. Distinguishing the things and processes of the world according to the categories of his or her awareness, the seeker would experience change and the resistance of change.

The finality of the world gives significance to experience. What is done cannot be undone later, what is left undone cannot later be accomplished. Yet the world also reflects the principle of variety and there is no limit to what may be experienced.

By the willingness to perceive and to experience, the seeker frees the self from limitation, and finds unbounded opportunity to learn and to become.

# 23
# PO
# SPLITTING
# APART

## STRUCTURE

Outer: The *Mountain*: Finality.
  Outer Nuclear: The *Receptive*: The principle of potentiation.
  Inner Nuclear: The *Receptive*: The principle of reality.
Inner: The *Receptive*: The priest.

## COMMENTARY

The priest, facing the unknown, feels the despair of separation and alienation from that which he or she would serve.

Knowing the limits of the self's receptiveness, the seeker knows also the finality of the moment which makes failure unalterable. Sensing the potentiality of the Void as it shapes the reality of the moment, the seeker can only acknowledge the self's unworthiness. Yet, in the mystery of potentiation lies the possibility of all becoming. In it, the seeker can reach for a more perfect priesthood, a more encompassing sacrifice, a more fulfilling duty. In the acceptance of failure there is opportunity to bear the burden of service.

Knowing imperfection, there is beginning.

# 24
# FU
# RETURN

Outer: The *Receptive*: Susceptibility.
  Outer Nuclear: The *Receptive*: The principle of potentiation.
  Inner Nuclear: The *Receptive*: The principle of reality.
  Inner: The *Arousal*: The intention to initiate.

## COMMENTARY

The shaman intends to originate as expression of receptivity and emptiness. Yet who is it that conceives what is to be initiated? Who is the dreamer?

The world is susceptible to action, yet, before the act, there was the thought that chose the action. What is originated is never exactly what was conceived. The concept rules the act but not its consequences. Out of the darkness of the unknown and unknowable, the new is summoned, but it is not ever what was defined or named. Therefore experience remains ever new, manifestation of unlimited potentiality.

In the experience the dreamer is renewed, recreating the dreamer that dreams the dreamer.

# 25

# WU WANG
# INNOCENCE
# (THE UNEXPECTED)

## STRUCTURE

Outer: The *Creative*: Imminence.
Outer Nuclear: The *Wood*: The principle of consistency.
Inner Nuclear: The *Mountain*: The intention to experience finality.
Inner: The *Arousal*: The intention to initiate.

## COMMENTARY

The shaman intends to originate in order to experience completion, finality. What is done cannot be undone. The act completes the intention and so demands accounting.

The world is imminent; it has a reality and an impact that cannot be denied. In this it obeys the principle of consistency as all things remain forever in harmony despite all becoming. The seeker too is within the harmony, as is the act. Therefore, the act of origination returns to impact the self, and the seeker becomes the effect of what was done.

The seeker may claim the purity of intention, denying responsibility for what occurs beyond expectation or desire. Yet, if so, it is a denial of the opportunity to learn and to become. The world is the arena for testing belief; there is no test if the seeker does not acknowledge the justice of experience.

# 26

# TA CH'U

# THE TAMING POWER OF THE GREAT

## STRUCTURE

Outer: The *Mountain*: Finality.
Outer Nuclear: The *Arousal*: The principle of uniqueness.
Inner Nuclear: The *Joyous*: The principle of assimilation.
Inner: The *Creative*: The shaman.

## COMMENTARY

The shaman acts, seeking to impose will upon the world. Accepting the need to assimilate the lessons of experience, he or she seeks to test the ways of power.

The finality of the world enforces the lessons of experience. The principle of uniqueness ensures the unboundedness of opportunity to learn. Yet the shaman must also acknowledge that what is done has effect, even when it fails the intent. Accepting responsibility for failure as for success, the seeker can learn the finality of what is done.

Accepting the limits of decision, the seeker can find the unboundedness of responsibility.

# 27

# I

# THE CORNERS
# OF THE MOUTH
# (NOURISHMENT)

## STRUCTURE

> Outer: The *Mountain*: Finality.
>> Outer Nuclear: The *Receptive*: The principle of potentiation.
>> Inner Nuclear: The *Receptive*: The principle of reality.
> Inner: The *Arousal*: The intention to initiate.

## COMMENTARY

The shaman intends to originate but can do so only according to the reality of the world and the strictures it imposes.

The finality of the world ensures the reality of what is done, preventing its undoing. What the seeker has originated came from the Void and the infinite potentiality that is there. Once born, it finds its own reality, separate from the desire or intention of its creator. The seeker must confront what was done, accepting its own reality, yet knowing his or her own connection to it. In the process, the seeker is recreated.

By the measure of the act and its consequences, the seeker chooses what will be the self recreated by the act.

# TA KUO
# PREPONDERANCE
# OF THE GREAT

## STRUCTURE

Outer: The *Joyous*: Continuity.
  Outer Nuclear: The *Creative*: The principle of autonomy.
  Inner Nuclear: The *Creative*: The intention to experience.
Inner: The *Wood*: Participation.

## COMMENTARY

The priest participates in a reality to which he or she is subordinate. By accepting that reality the seeker admits experience, for it is only through acceptance that meaning can be found.

The world moves continuously as the present flows out of the past and forms the basis of the future. As events occur within the world's autonomy, they may acquire significance for the seeker as they impact his or her life. In this impact, the seeker discovers reality and the lessons of experience are enforced.

The reality the seeker sees is not the whole for none can comprehend the world's totality while still within it. The reality that is unnamed will ultimately test all boundaries. In the end, the experience of subordination itself must be transformed and its barriers transcended.

# 29

# K'AN

# THE ABYSMAL
# (WATER)

## STRUCTURE

Outer: The *Abyss*: The flux of change.
    Outer Nuclear: The *Mountain*: The principle of finality.
    Inner Nuclear: The *Arousal*: The intention to experience origination.
Inner: The *Abyss*: The intention to control.

## COMMENTARY

The shaman seeks to exercise control through the power of origination. In origination, there is the power to initiate what will oppose the unwanted or will further what is desired. In the power of origination, then, there is the path to control.

Yet there is danger in origination, for none can know with precision what has been originated. The world is in continual change as flows intersect with flows and processes ceaselessly reshape themselves. The act of origination creates new turbulence and new dangers, compounding those the seeker would control. The seeker, if wise, may see the threat of danger as a test of beingness. By acceptance of the limits on the power to control danger, the seeker affirms his or her identity.

In the affirmation of action, there may be sensed the self that lies within the central quiet, unmoved by the illusion of danger.

# 30

# LI

# THE FIRE
# (THE CLINGING)

## STRUCTURE

Outer: The *Fire*: Lawfulness.
  Outer Nuclear: The *Joyous*: The principle of comprehensibility.
  Inner Nuclear: The *Wood*: The principle of involvement.
Inner: The *Fire*: Perception.

## COMMENTARY

The priest contemplates the diversity of the world. The perception that makes contemplation possible depends on a separation that gives perspective. Yet, this isolation does not deny the involvement without which the perception would be without substance.

The world around the seeker is lawful, though the fullness of the Law is beyond all comprehension. Contemplating the world, the priest can still reach a partial understanding. What is grasped may be but a small part of the Law, and even that may be clouded by misconception. Yet what is understood offers a basis for further contemplation and a foundation from which to seek a deeper, less mistaken, understanding.

In the willingness to seek comprehension, the seeker allows the self to be involved. In being willing to experience the Law despite the errors and insufficiency of perception, he or she allows the self to be.

# CHAPTER VII

# THE HEXAGRAMS: BOOK 2

As indicated at the start of Chapter VI, it is traditional to separate the sequence of hexagrams into two "books," one with hexagrams 1 through 30, the other with the remaining hexagrams 31 through 64.

At the start of Chapter VI, we sketched in very briefly what we believe is the significance of this separation. While that view is based on interpreting the hexagrams from a rather different point of view than that considered here, the student can perhaps see echoes of it here. For the most part, the hexagrams of Book 2 seem to probe somewhat more deeply into the psyche of the querent and are less concerned with the specific way the querent should address the problem. The difference is not fundamental in this interpretation, but it is there.

In any case, we have chosen to preserve the separation and accordingly have divided the entire sequence into two chapters.

# 31
# HSIEN
# INFLUENCE
# (WOOING)

## STRUCTURE

Outer: The *Joyous*: Continuity.
  Outer Nuclear: The *Creative*: The principle of autonomy.
  Inner Nuclear: The *Wood*: The principle of involvement.
Inner: The *Mountain*: The intention to terminate.

## COMMENTARY

The shaman intends to terminate what has existed. In the process, the seeker acknowledges his or her involvement with the world and confirms its importance.

The world has its own continuity as its present arises from the past and makes possible the future. The shaman's actions affect the world as events within the world's reality, taking part within its continuity. So also is the decision to act a consequence of the context in which the seeker moves.

It is not by action that the seeker affirms selfhood, nor even by decision. Rather, it is by the awareness of involvement and the acceptance of the world's influence on those decisions and actions. Thus can the seeker know self.

# 32
# HÊNG
# DURATION

STRUCTURE

Outer: The *Arousal*: Unpredictability.
Outer Nuclear: The *Joyous*: The principle of comprehensibility.
Inner Nuclear: The *Creative*: The intention to experience.
Inner: The *Wood*: Participation.

COMMENTARY

The priest, participating in the manifest reality, finds an unpredictable world. Seeking experience, its unexpectedness gives the seeker freedom to discover.

Despite its unpredictability, the world is somewhat comprehensible. Observing what is visible and assessing what can be seen according to his or her understanding, the priest can find meaning even in the unknown and the unexpected. The path to knowing is long; errors and incompleteness in understanding persist. Yet intention is fulfilled by the effort.

Recognizing the instant within eternity, the seeker finds the substance of becoming.

# 33

# TUN

# RETREAT

## STRUCTURE

Outer: The *Creative*: Imminence.
Outer Nuclear: The *Creative*: The principle of autonomy.
Inner Nuclear: The *Wood*: The principle of involvement.
Inner: The *Mountain*: The intention to terminate.

## COMMENTARY

The shaman intends to end what has been begun. The decision acknowledges his or her subordination to the world and its reality.

The world is imminent; it has an impact that cannot be denied and manifests an autonomy that ever lies beyond the seeker's grasp. Being involved, the shaman can only act within a context whose fullness cannot ever be fully understood.

In the intention to complete, the seeker does not deny the world or its reality. Rather, the decision is a recognition of the world's reality. The seeker acknowledges that all action is shaped by the world and its autonomous reality, yet responsibility remains. By action, then, the seeker validates the reality of the self's involvement.

# TA CHUANG
# THE POWER OF THE GREAT

## STRUCTURE

Outer: The *Arousal*: Unpredictability.
Outer Nuclear: The *Joyous*: The principle of comprehensibility.
Inner Nuclear: The *Creative*: The intention to experience.
Inner: The *Creative*: The shaman.

## COMMENTARY

The shaman acts, seeking to shape the world according to his or her will, fulfilling the intention to experience and test the limits of power.

The world is unpredictable. Despite the shaman's will, it must be acknowledged that all acts have consequences beyond all desire or expectations. Using experience to guide comprehension, the shaman can partially understand what he or she has done, but never completely. There remains forever the opportunity to learn more. There is ever the opportunity for new experience.

Defining the purpose as the fulfillment of will, the shaman must fail. Seeking instead to experience the power of will and to test its nature and limits, there is success.

# 35

# CHIN

# PROGRESS

Outer: The *Fire*: Lawfulness.
Outer Nuclear: The *Abyss*: The principle of change.
Inner Nuclear: The *Mountain*: The intention to experience finality.
Inner: The *Receptive*: The priest.

## COMMENTARY

The priest bows before the Law that rules the world. Seeking to experience finality, the seeker contemplates the unknown and the unknowable. It must be so, for completions summon the unknown from the depths of the unknowable.

The world is the expression and fulfillment of the Law and so remains forever lawful. Under the Law, the world is ever changing. Yet who can comprehend its processes? Who can know the fullness of the Law? While still within the world, the priest cannot ever fully understand. Yet, in the growth of experience, the seeker also finds the way to diminish ignorance and insufficiency.

In the contemplation of the unknown and by acknowledging the unknowable, the priest can learn something of the nature of sacrifice and of the reasons for the self's acceptance.

# 36

# MING I

# DARKENING
# OF THE LIGHT

## STRUCTURE

Outer: The *Receptive*: Susceptibility.
Outer Nuclear: The *Arousal*: The principle of uniqueness.
Inner Nuclear: The *Abyss*: The intention to experience control.
Inner: The *Fire*: Perception.

## COMMENTARY

The priest contemplates the world, perceiving distinctions between the myriad things and processes. In the process, the seeker observes the patterns of change and the dance of reality.

The world is susceptible to the seeker; it is changed by his or her presence and by what is done or left undone. Yet the consequences of each act remain unknown for the world is ever new and unique. Even in the appearance of similarity there are always differences that have effects beyond the limits of perception. Therefore the priest remains bound by the limits of awareness. But therefore also, the seeker may know the need to pass beyond those limits.

# 37

# CHIA JÊN

# THE FAMILY
# (THE CLAN)

## STRUCTURE

Outer: The *Wood*: Integrity.
Outer Nuclear: The *Fire*: The principle of lawfulness.
Inner Nuclear: The *Abyss*: The intention to experience control.
Inner: The *Fire*: Perception.

## COMMENTARY

The priest perceives the myriad things and processes of the world and makes distinctions between them, categorizing the world of experience. Thus the seeker is able to experience change and to discover intimations of the Law that governs change.

The world the priest contemplates has its own integrity. It is indeed lawful but the Law it manifests is its own, ever beyond the seeker's comprehension. The seeker too is within the world, a part within its wholeness and so governed by its Law. So too are the illusions of the seeker's perception.

In the search for final understanding, the seeker must fail. Yet, in the process, the seeker finds the categories of his or her own beingness, and of the process of becoming. In this the seeker need not fail.

# 38
# K'UEI
# OPPOSITION

STRUCTURE

Outer: The *Fire*: Lawfulness.
Outer Nuclear: The *Abyss*: The principle of change.
Inner Nuclear: The *Fire*: The principle of discrimination.
Inner: The *Joyous*: Acceptance.

COMMENTARY

As priest, the seeker becomes open to experience and allows the self to learn. Yet care is needed. By discriminating among events to decide which are significant and which trivial, the seeker implicitly chooses what may be learned.

The world is lawful despite the continual flux of change and becoming, but the fullness of the Law is beyond all knowing. Not knowing what consequences may emerge, the seeker may fear the processes of the world. Yet fear denies acceptance. It tempts the seeker to dismiss the unknown as irrelevant, a distraction from the business of living. Or becoming obsessed with fear, the seeker may recognize only the uncertainty and so miss the lessons of what can be known.

By acceptance of the unknown Law that governs change, the priest learns to accept self also. Even as the seeker cannot know the fullness of the Law, neither can he or she know the fullness of the inner law that governs the self's own changes. Claiming the acceptance of the priest, the seeker can only bow before the self's own becoming.

# 39
# CHIEN
# OBSTRUCTION

## STRUCTURE

Outer: The *Abyss*: The flux of change.
Outer Nuclear: The *Fire*: The principle of lawfulness.
Inner Nuclear: The *Abyss*: The intention to experience control.
Inner: The *Mountain*: The intention to terminate.

## COMMENTARY

The shaman intends to terminate, seeking the experience of control. Control is best achieved, to whatever extent it is, by the prevention of what otherwise might have happened.

The world is ever in flux as its processes drive continual change. Yet it remains lawful though the seeker cannot know the fullness of its Law. In the errors and incompleteness of understanding, the shaman cannot find the total control that is sought. Even the goal of ending what is no longer seen as appropriate seems uncertain. The goal can be redefined to promote achievability, but often only at the expense of the deeper purpose of the self.

Seeking control, the shaman ultimately fails. Yet, by the effort, the seeker makes possible the self's own becoming; it is the failure that summons forth the effort.

## STRUCTURE

Outer: The *Arousal*: Unpredictability.
Outer Nuclear: The *Abyss*: The principle of change.
Inner Nuclear: The *Fire*: The principle of discrimination.
Inner: The *Abyss*: The intention to control.

## COMMENTARY

The shaman intends to exercise control. Toward this end, discrimination is important for none can hope to control the whole of the environment or know the full effect of what is done.

The world is unpredictable, manifesting the principle of change in all its elements and aspects. Therefore the shaman can alter the world, but cannot ever know with certainty what will be the consequences. Doing what is judged useful, the seeker learns the value and also the limits both of judgment and of control over what will be.

In judging action, the seeker must stand apart from the doing and its consequences. Then, acknowledging ignorance, the seeker can quietly contemplate the flux of change and so seek to reduce ignorance.

# 41

# SUN

# DECREASE

## STRUCTURE

Outer: The *Mountain*: Finality.
Outer Nuclear: The *Receptive*: The principle of potentiation.
Inner Nuclear: The *Arousal*: The intention to experience origination.
Inner: The *Joyous*: Acceptance.

## COMMENTARY

The priest is acceptive in order to test the nature of origination. By acknowledging the consequences of what has been originated and the reality of the trial, the seeker creates the possibility of learning.

The finality of the world gives value to experience. It ensures that what is done cannot be undone, and what is not done cannot later be performed. Yet, beyond the finality, there is the principle of potentiation. The past cannot be changed, but the future contains all possibility. What is originated arises out of that potentiality. By the acceptance of experience, the seeker tests the self's own potentiality.

By acceptance, the seeker confronts his or her own unknowingness, and so acknowledges the burden of priesthood. Thus does the seeker allow the self's becoming.

# INCREASE

## STRUCTURE

Outer: The *Wood*: Integrity.
Outer Nuclear: The *Mountain*: The principle of finality.
Inner Nuclear: The *Receptive*: The principle of reality.
Inner: The *Arousal*: The intention to initiate.

## COMMENTARY

The shaman intends to originate. What is originated must be in accordance with the principle of reality. To succeed, the shaman must accept being bound to the possible and to the reality of the moment.

The world has its own integrity, its own wholeness. The act of origination cannot violate this integrity for it is within the whole. The world enforces this truth through the finality that closes the past from further change or influence. What exists must be appropriate to what has been, even as it limits what may come to be. Therefore the shaman originates, but what is originated becomes part within the world, shaped by the world's integrity.

Confronting the uncertainty of doing and the unknown consequences of what is done, the seeker confronts reality. By the trial, the shaman tests also his or her own reality, seeking to discover the self's potential.

# 43

# KUAI .

# BREAKTHROUGH
# (RESOLUTENESS)

## STRUCTURE

Outer: The *Joyous*: Continuity.
   Outer Nuclear: The *Creative*: The principle of autonomy.
   Inner Nuclear: The *Creative*: The intention to experience.
Inner: The *Creative*: The shaman.

## COMMENTARY

The shaman seeks to impose his or her will upon the environment, seeking to experience and to test the nature and extent of power and responsibility.

The shaman, however, cannot break the continuity of the world as the present flows out of the past and the future from the present. The shaman may claim the power of intention but he or she, too, is within the world, bound to its continuity and within its autonomy.

What then is the nature of will? It exists within the intentionality of the self. The act that manifests the will is not the will. The shaman acts within the world, but remains always responsible to self.

# 44

# KOU

# COMING TO MEET

## STRUCTURE

Outer: The *Creative*: Imminence.
  Outer Nuclear: The *Creative*: The principle of autonomy.
  Inner Nuclear: The *Creative*: The intention to experience.
Inner: The *Wood*: Participation.

## COMMENTARY

The priest participates in the world and so fulfills the intention to experience.

The world is imminent; it has an impact that cannot be denied without denying existence itself. Its lessons are not ignorable with impunity no matter how harsh the teaching may appear. The harshness is a consequence of the world's autonomy that may seem to deny even the seeker's existence. The world is not malicious, but neither does it acknowledge the importance of the priest. It is the seeker who has sought the world, looking to experience what it offers.

In the face of the uncaring world, the seeker is driven to find validity within the self. Confronting the opacity of the world, the seeker can only turn inward. There may be discovered the self that, by experiencing, asserts its own existence and value.

# 45

# TS'UI

# GATHERING TOGETHER (MASSING)

Outer: The *Joyous*: Continuity.
Outer Nuclear: The *Wood*: The principle of consistency.
Inner Nuclear: The *Mountain*: The intention to experience finality.
Inner: The *Receptive*: The priest.

## COMMENTARY

The priest bows before the sacrificial altar, fulfilling the intention to experience finality. Accepting the opportunity of existence, the seeker endures the finality that gives substance to experience.

The world the priest serves has continuity—the present flows out of the past and is the foundation of the future. In the flow of time there is the principle of consistency as the separate elements of the whole interact to maintain the whole. In the finality of the present, the priest finds the challenge of acceptance. In the closure of what is past its time, there is the measure of the beingness that is ever within the moment.

# 46
# SHÊNG
# PUSHING UPWARD

## STRUCTURE

Outer: The *Receptive*: Susceptibility.
Outer Nuclear: The *Arousal*: The principle of uniqueness.
Inner Nuclear: The *Joyous*: The principle of assimilation.
Inner: The *Wood*: Participation.

## COMMENTARY

The priest participates in the world, accepting subordination in order to assimilate experience. It is only within an environment that exceeds the reach of understanding that the unknown offers experience to be assimilated.

The world is susceptible to the seeker's presence; it responds to what is done, though often not according to the seeker's desire or expectation. Within the world, there is the possibility of the new—expression of the uniqueness of the moment. Therefore, the seeker's acts can evoke what otherwise would not be. Yet what is evoked must have been within the potentiality of existence.

By the subordination that is part of priesthood, the seeker discovers the potential both for what furthers and what does not. So may responsibility be learned and the duty to seek the limits of perfectibility discovered.

# 47

# K'UN

# OPPRESSION
# (EXHAUSTION)

STRUCTURE

> Outer: The *Joyous*: Continuity.
>> Outer Nuclear: The *Wood*: The principle of consistency.
>> Inner Nuclear: The *Fire*: The principle of discrimination.
> Inner: The *Abyss*: The intention to control.

COMMENTARY

The shaman intends to control. Toward this goal, discrimination is necessary to identify the separate aspects and elements of the situation. Otherwise, the seeker could not name what is to be controlled or decide what might serve the goal.

The world has continuity, expression of its self-consistency. The seeker acts within this world and is not separate from it. Therefore, what is done is bound also by the world's flow for the seeker's acts arise from the past and condition the future. Even the seeker's decisions are consequences of experience and past desire. What then is the meaning of intention?

The shaman decides and acts but, before the decision, there was the intention to decide. Behind the will to experience and to test the power of decision, there is the self that wills. In the recognition of the limits of possibility in the world, the seeker may find the pattern of the self's reality and know its inward self-consistency.

# 48

# CHING

# THE WELL

## STRUCTURE

Outer: The *Abyss*: The flux of change.
Outer Nuclear: The *Fire*: The principle of lawfulness.
Inner Nuclear: The *Joyous*: The principle of assimilation.
Inner: The *Wood*: Participation.

## COMMENTARY

The priest has chosen to participate within the world in order to assimilate experience. Assimilation becomes possible only within a larger context that, though unknown and ultimately unknowable, yet provides a framework for experience.

The world is ever changing. Behind all change, there is the Law that governs change. The priest cannot know the fullness of the Law, but its presence can be sensed and its substance sought. It is only through the world's lawfulness that experience can be meaningful. Without it, there would only be a chaos that must deny becoming.

Experiencing the world, the seeker learns. In the learning, he or she may grow beyond the context the self conceived when it accepted participation. Yet there is no limit; there remains always the larger community, the more open context, leading ultimately only to the unbounded context of the Law itself.

# 49

# KO

# REVOLUTION
# (MOLTING)

## STRUCTURE

> Outer: The *Joyous*: Continuity.
>   Outer Nuclear: The *Creative*: The principle of autonomy.
>   Inner Nuclear: The *Wood*: The principle of involvement.
> Inner: The *Fire*: Perception.

## COMMENTARY

The priest contemplates the world, distinguishing the separate things and flows within it that are perceivable. In this, the self's involvement with the world is acknowledged, and the seeker becomes aware of the self's own presence in the world.

The world is continuous as the present evolves from the past and provides the basis of the future. It is this continuity that gives order to its autonomy, linking one moment to the next. The seeker, too, is within this process. The priest contemplates the flow of time, yet remains inseparably involved in it. In the apparent contradiction, the seeker has the opportunity to search for understanding and to discover self.

# TING

# THE CALDRON

## STRUCTURE

Outer: The *Fire*: Lawfulness.
Outer Nuclear: The *Joyous*: The principle of comprehensibility.
Inner Nuclear: The *Creative*: The intention to experience.
Inner: The *Wood*: Participation.

## COMMENTARY

The priest participates in the world of his or her awareness. The role is accepted in order to experience, for a context is need in which to examine the consequences of what is done and who the doer is.

The world is lawful. Although the Law it manifests is beyond understanding, unknowable in its full expression, its workings can be perceived in part and with some error. Therefore, it can be comprehended, albeit always incompletely and with error. It is this that makes it possible to assimilate experience and to learn.

As the errors of the past are accepted and considered, understanding can grow, allowing the seeker to move beyond the world of his or her past experiencing. Then can awareness expand, reaching for a new and greater understanding.

# 51

# CHÊN

# THE AROUSING
# (SHOCK, THUNDER)

## STRUCTURE

Outer: The *Arousal*: Unpredictability.
Outer Nuclear: The *Abyss*: The principle of change.
Inner Nuclear: The *Mountain*: The intention to experience finality.
Inner: The *Arousal*: The intention to initiate.

## COMMENTARY

The shaman intends to originate in order to experience completion. In completion there is the basis of the new as what is ended is replaced by what has not yet been.

The world is unpredictable as it manifests change in every detail. The shaman, originating according to intention, cannot know what has been initiated since what is originated must change as it takes its place within the world of change. The originator cannot know what it will become, and will not find it becoming what was desired or expected. As it evolves, it bears witness to what the seeker does not see, showing the effect of forces the seeker does not know or understand.

If the shaman demands conformance to the original desire or expectation, he or she will be confounded and so lose the opportunity to learn. However, contemplating what happens and accepting full responsibility for it, the seeker may discover something of his or her own becoming.

# 52
# KÊN
# KEEPING STILL
# (MOUNTAIN)

## STRUCTURE

Outer: The *Mountain*: Finality.
  Outer Nuclear: The *Arousal*: The principle of uniqueness.
  Inner Nuclear: The *Abyss*: The intention to experience control.
Inner: The *Mountain*: The intention to terminate.

## COMMENTARY

The shaman intends to terminate what has been. He or she seeks in this way to experience change; the most certain way to change the world is through terminating what was.

The world has finality—what is done cannot be undone, what is not done cannot be later done—a consequence of the eternal newness of the world that ensures that the past is not recoverable. Therefore, what the shaman does has significance. What is terminated cannot ever be reborn exactly as it was and the shaman's action is irredeemable. Deciding an action was in error, the fault cannot be recovered in full. The seeker may delude himself or herself by choosing to ignore what contradicts desire. If so, the seeker only denies experience and limits the opportunity to become.

# 53

# CHIEN

# DEVELOPMENT
# (GRADUAL PROGRESS)

## STRUCTURE

> Outer: The *Wood*: Integrity.
>> Outer Nuclear: The *Fire*: The principle of lawfulness.
>> Inner Nuclear: The *Abyss*: The intention to experience control.
> Inner: The *Mountain*: The intention to terminate.

## COMMENTARY

The shaman intends to terminate what has existed. He or she would experience the control that is best accomplished by the ending of what is counter to desire.

The world has its own integrity, expression of the underlying Law that governs its existence. Inviolable, the world is not shaken by the shaman's acts for they too are within the world's integrity. The shaman, intending to experience control, must learn to act in deliberate accord with that integrity. Exerting power to end what does not further, the shaman allows the world to accomplish what is sought as part of the processes that maintain integrity. So, by small steps, is the goal achieved.

Thus does the seeker learn to use the interplay between freedom of purpose and the binding of the Law to fulfill intention. In the process, the seeker acknowledges his or her own beingness on the path of becoming.

# 54
# KUEI MEI
# THE MARRYING MAIDEN

Outer: The *Arousal*: Unpredictability.
  Outer Nuclear: The *Abyss*: The principle of change.
  Inner Nuclear: The *Fire*: The principle of discrimination.
Inner: The *Joyous*: Acceptance.

COMMENTARY

The priest accepts the reality of experiencing, seeking to understand its significance. By the power of discrimination, the priest searches for what is to be served and for ways to accept the lessons of experience.

The world is unpredictable as it manifests the principle of change. All things, all processes change in ways the seeker cannot know in full. Therefore experience remains unbounded, and the priest is ever challenged to accept the new. Yet discrimination implies the distance that allows perspective; the judgment of significance denies the acceptance that is unqualified.

Both separation and acceptance are needed to know experience. Yet the illusion of separation denies acceptance, while acceptance prevents discrimination and disables judgment. In the end, the lessons of reality must enforce transcendence and opposites must be resolved.

# 55
# FÊNG
# ABUNDANCE
# (FULLNESS)

## STRUCTURE

> Outer: The *Arousal*: Unpredictability.
> Outer Nuclear: The *Joyous*: The principle of comprehensibility.
> Inner Nuclear: The *Wood*: The principle of involvement.
> Inner: The *Fire*: Perception.

## COMMENTARY

The priest perceives the diversity of the world. In so doing, the seeker acknowledges involvement, for it is this that gives significance to what is seen.

The world is unpredictable, yet it remains comprehensible within the limits of the seeker's understanding. Perception and understanding are always incomplete and only partially correct, yet they are sufficient for contemplation. They support the search for a greater vision and a new understanding. Building on error, the priest may approach truth. Accepting the limits of understanding, the seeker can expand the vision that seeks to encompass the whole.

If the final truth must ever remain hidden while the seeker moves within the world, there is still opportunity to search and, in the process, to learn something of self.

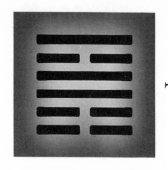

# 56
# LÜ
# THE WANDERER

## STRUCTURE

Outer: The *Fire*: Lawfulness.
Outer Nuclear: The *Joyous*: The principle of comprehensibility.
Inner Nuclear: The *Wood*: The principle of involvement.
Inner: The *Mountain*: The intention to terminate.

## COMMENTARY

The shaman intends to terminate and so to manifest the self's involvement with the world. Without that involvement, the act would be without significance, an empty move in a meaningless game.

The world in which the shaman acts is lawful although the Law cannot ever be fully comprehended while the seeker remains involved. Yet, despite the limits on understanding, the world is still somewhat comprehensible. The errors of belief and the incompleteness of understanding do not prevent action—the shaman can still know purpose and pursue expectation. Therefore error can be discovered and understanding improved.

By acknowledging the errors of action and understanding, the seeker allows the self to accept a deeper understanding and a greater challenge to learn and to become.

# 57

# SUN

# THE GENTLE
# (THE WIND,
# THE PENETRATING)

STRUCTURE

> Outer: The *Wood*: Integrity.
> > Outer Nuclear: The *Fire*: The principle of lawfulness.
> > Inner Nuclear: The *Joyous*: The principle of assimilation.
> Inner: The *Wood*: Participation.

COMMENTARY

The priest accepts participation in the world. By doing so, he or she allows the self to assimilate experience and so to grow through participation.

The world has its own integrity that is independent of the seeker, expression of a Law that is beyond all knowing. The priest, by participating, becomes part of that integrity, bound also by its Law. Though the fullness of the Law cannot ever be known while the priest remains within the world, still, by acceptance, there is opened the path to seeking and to the assimilation of the reality that can be identified and accepted.

The seeker, intending to further what is needed, fulfills the self.

# 58
# TUI
# THE JOYOUS
# (THE LAKE)

## STRUCTURE

Outer: The *Joyous*: Continuity.
Outer Nuclear: The *Wood*: The principle of consistency.
Inner Nuclear: The *Fire*: The principle of discrimination.
Inner: The *Joyous*: Acceptance.

## COMMENTARY

The priest accepts the strictures of the world, allowing the self to be the effect of the environment. By this, the variety of the world is acknowledged and opportunity provided for discrimination.

The world is continuous as events flow out of the past and shape the future. Despite all change, it remains ever self-consistent, not swayed by the seeker's desires or expectations. The priest, accepting this, allows the self to be an element within that flow, embedded in its consistency. Yet, though contained within the processes of the world, the seeker can still contemplate the nature and purpose of acceptance.

In the serenity of contemplation, the seeker may touch the self that, itself unchanging, accepts becoming.

# 59

# HUAN

# DISPERSION
# (DISSOLUTION)

STRUCTURE

> Outer: The *Wood*: Integrity.
> Outer Nuclear: The *Mountain*: The principle of finality.
> Inner Nuclear: The *Arousal*: The intention to experience origination.
> Inner: The *Abyss*: The intention to control.

COMMENTARY

The shaman seeks to control the environment in order to experience origination. By control, it becomes possible to know what has been originated, and to contemplate the consequences of the act.

The world has its own integrity that is independent of the seeker's intention. In this it expresses the principle of finality that closes the past, isolating it from all desire or will. The shaman, having initiated, cannot change what has been done; what was originated becomes what it must within the world's integrity. The seeker can only contemplate the consequences, seeking to learn what may be known.

The seeker, too, is within the integrity of the world and therefore also becomes what is necessary. The seeker's past must also be accepted for it, too, cannot be altered. By the exercise of control, the seeker alters only what the self may become.

# 60

# CHIEH

# LIMITATION

## STRUCTURE

Outer: The *Abyss*: The flux of change.
  Outer Nuclear: The *Mountain*: The principle of finality.
  Inner Nuclear: The *Arousal*: The intention to experience origination.
  Inner: The *Joyous*: Acceptance.

## COMMENTARY

The seeker, as priest, accepts the strictures of the environment in order to experience origination. What he or she can originate must always be compatible with the reality of its existence.

The world is ever changing as its flows compound with themselves, influencing all things within it. In this flux, the world exhibits finality; the past is closed by the present, and the present dies within the moment. The seeker, too, is immersed within this flux, and so must ever change. In contemplating the world and accepting the consequences of his or her presences and actions, the seeker may see the reflection of his or her inner beingness and becomingness.

# 61

# CHUNG FU
# INNER TRUTH

## STRUCTURE

Outer: The *Wood*: Integrity.
Outer Nuclear: The *Mountain*: The principle of finality.
Inner Nuclear: The *Arousal*: The intention to experience origination.
Inner: The *Joyous*: Acceptance.

## COMMENTARY

The priest accepts the domination of the world of experience in order to test the power of origination. That world is necessary since there is need for an environment in which to judge the consequences of decision.

The world has its own integrity, independent of the seeker's desires or intentions. It is this that allows experience to teach as action leads to unexpected consequences. The world's integrity is expression of the principle of finality—ensuring that what is done cannot be undone, what is left undone cannot later be corrected. So is experience given significance and the lessons of reality their importance.

The seeker, accepting the reality and substance of experience, allows the self to learn and so become. Thus is there acceptance of the self that seeks becoming.

# HSIAO KUO

# PREPONDERANCE OF THE SMALL

## STRUCTURE

Outer: The *Arousal*: Unpredictability.
    Outer Nuclear: The *Joyous*: The principle of comprehensibility.
    Inner Nuclear: The *Wood*: The principle of involvement.
Inner: The *Mountain*: The intention to terminate.

## COMMENTARY

The shaman intends to end what has existed. In this, he or she fulfills the implications of the self's involvement and seeks to learn how to further what is needed.

The world is unpredictable, though somewhat comprehensible. The seeker's understanding is ever incomplete and partially in error, yet it can guide action. Knowing the limitations of understanding, the shaman does not seek to command what shall be. Instead, will is focused on the ending of what does not further, and so accepts that the world will flow according to its own harmony.

By the acknowledgment of error and the acceptance of unknowingness, the seeker finds the path to the self's unbinding.

# 63

# CHI CHI
# AFTER
# COMPLETION

## STRUCTURE

> Outer: The *Abyss*: The flux of change.
>> Outer Nuclear: The *Fire*: The principle of lawfulness.
>> Inner Nuclear: The *Abyss*: The intention to experience control.
> Inner: The *Fire*: Perception.

## COMMENTARY

The priest perceives the myriad things and processes of the world. Seeking to experience control, he or she stands before the infinite variety of possibility.

The world is ever changing, as are all its separate things and processes. Yet it is also lawful, although the Law cannot be fully comprehended while the seeker remains within it. Knowing self to be within the eternal flux of change, the seeker can indeed experience some degree of control. Yet action cannot control the whole, nor indefinitely control any part. The variety of the universe must eventually escape all effort.

Seeking control, the seeker must eventually fail. Seeking the experience of control and the lessons it may offer, the priest must eventually find what is needed.

# 64

# WEI CHI

# BEFORE COMPLETION

## STRUCTURE

>Outer: The *Fire*: Lawfulness.
>Outer Nuclear: The *Abyss*: The principle of change.
>Inner Nuclear: The *Fire*: The principle of discrimination.
>Inner: The *Abyss*: The intention to control.

## COMMENTARY

The shaman intends to exercise control, testing the limits of the principle of discrimination.

The world is lawful, although the fullness of the Law cannot be known while the seeker remains subordinate to it. Yet the Law exists; it governs the flux of change that pervades the world.

The shaman, exercising the intention to control, can only act within the Law. Perceiving the consequences of what is done, the shaman may recognize the failure of intention and so learn something of the limits of understanding. By the intention, then, he or she seeks to perfect understanding. So is there a commitment to the self's becomng.

Contemplating the effort of control and the processes of change, the seeker can discover something of the inner Law that rules the self's becoming.

# CHAPTER IX

# THE TRIGRAMS

In this chapter, we develop the interpretation of the trigrams that is summarized in Table 3 of Chapter VI. The interpretation is based on the shaman-priest duality discussed in Chapter V.

As has been indicated, the trigrams occur in four positions in a hexagram: the Inner Trigram at the bottom, then the Inner Nuclear one, the Outer Nuclear one, and, at the top, the Outer Trigram. While the interpretation of the trigrams varies according to position, they have a generic meaning that is essentially independent of position. This meaning is developed from the family arrangement given in Table 2, Chapter III, The Family Arrangement.

## GENERIC INTERPRETATION

We have already associated the trigram of the Creative with the shaman as he or she seeks to shape the world. Generically, it signifies the source of influence without regard for intention or even for what the actual effect may be.

This can be summarized as follows:

*CH'IEN*, The Creative:

The yang principle. The source of influence and effect.

An active influence can (a) seek to create something new, (b) seek to modify or maintain what already exists, or (c) seek to terminate what exists. These three categories are symbolized by the three sons in the family arrangement, the three lesser yang trigrams:

*CHÊN*, The Arousal:

Beginning. The source of a flow that creates something new.

*K'AN*, The Abyss:

Change. The source of a flow that changes something, or resists change.

*KÊN*, The Mountain:

Ending. The source of a flow that completes or destroys something.

These categories are subjective, dependent on a point of view. If something new is created, its presence changes the situation. It also ends those aspects of the situation that are replaced by the new. Similarly, if something is changed, this creates a new situation and ends the old. Again, if something is ended, this creates a new condition and changes the general situation. The three categories are intimately linked and philosophically intertwined. Nevertheless, the categorization is useful when dealing with human problems.

It is also worth emphasizing that the notion of a flow as being the cause of an effect is also a gross oversimplification. It is implicit in the I Ching that causal explanations are always incomplete if not false. What happens occurs within the totality of existence; it does not have any single, isolated cause. However, again the simplification is useful when dealing with human problems.

In the yin trigrams, now, we start with the trigram of the Receptive which we have already associated with the priest, particularly as he or she remains receptive to influences from a greater source. The generic meaning, then, concerns the state of being influenced by some flow without regard for the type of influence being exerted. We summarize this as follows:

*K'UN*, The Receptive:

The yin principle. The receptivity that accepts influence.

As with the yang conditions, there are three broad categories that can be distinguished. An influence can (a) create a new connection which leads to recognition of the source as an identifiable element, (b) provide information about the source and its influence, and (c) provide evidence of a greater whole in which the source and the target are both elements. We associate these characterizations with the three lesser yin trigrams:

*SUN*, The Wood or Wind:

Relatedness, participation, connection. The principle of interaction.

*LI*, The Fire, Clarity:

Categorization, particularization, description. The principle of discrimination.

*TUI*, The Joyous:

Unity, wholeness, completeness. The principle of interdependence.

Again, these categories are subjective, dependent on the point of view. They depend, also, on the illusions of the distinction between source and target, and the causality of influence. These illusions are necessary, at least as useful conventions, for the seeker to profit from experience or even know experience as relevant to his or her seeking.

# THE INNER TRIGRAMS

The generic meanings of the trigrams are specialized according to position. We consider, first, the Inner position. As indicated, this trigram symbolizes the questioner, the person who is confronting a problem. It classifies his or her intentions or attitudes, or what they should or might be. In terms of the primary duality, the yang trigrams refer to the shamanic role, the yin trigrams to the priest's. We summarize this view as follows, first for the yang trigrams:

*CH'IEN*, The Creative:

The shaman. The seeker's intention to influence his or her environment.

The lesser yang trigrams can be summarized as follows:

*CHÊN*, The Arousal:

The shamanic intention to initiate, to begin, to create something new.

*K'AN*, The Abyss:

The shamanic intention to control, seeking to change or to resist change.

*KÊN*, The Mountain:

The shamanic intention to terminate, to end, to close what has existed.

For the yin trigrams in the Inner position, we can write:

*K'UN*, The Receptive:

The priest as he accepts influence from another source, known or unknown.

For the lesser yin trigrams, we can summarize their significances as follows:

*SUN*, The Wood or Wind:

Participation as the priest accepts subordination to an external source.

*LI*, The Fire or Clarity:

Perception or discrimination through which the priest characterizes an influence.

*TUI*, The Joyous:

Acceptance as the priest recognizes the whole implied by the influence.

This completes the description of the trigrams in the Inner position.

## THE OUTER TRIGRAMS

Moving now to the Outer trigrams, these symbolize the seeker's environment in which he or she recognizes a problem. It symbolizes also the other pole of the flow of influence. Again, the generic interpretations of the trigrams need to be specialized. In this position, we do not have the duality to guide us except as we confront another individual who may take the role of shaman or priest, or as we personify the problem. More accurately, the issue is one of the character of the flow itself, rather than the state or purpose of its source. Nevertheless, we can find appropriate characterizations of the trigrams that match the generic interpretations and are consistent with their meanings in the Inner position.

For Ch'ien, we write the following:

*CH'IEN*, The Creative:

**The imminence of the world that gives impact to experience.**

Imminence, here, refers to the special quality of the world (the world that is the environment of the question) that gives its events impact. There are worlds that are not imminent—the worlds of fantasy, imagination, and dreams. In them, we can pursue intention and action. In them, we can and do test out alternatives. But, in the "real" world, we must live with the results. The world of our imagination is of true value, but it is only in the "real" world that we learn the hard lessons of experience..

Passing to the three lesser yang trigrams, these characterize the types of flows from the world that contribute to our problem:

*CHÊN*, The Arousal:

**Unpredictability, and the unexpectedness of events.**

*K'AN*, The Abyss:

**The unending flux of change within the world.**

*KÊN*, The Mountain:

**The finality of the world as time destroys the opportunities of the present.**

These qualities express the impact the world can have on our experience. Chên gives the opportunity to experience since the world is ever new. K'an gives content to experience as it drives change and becomingness. Kên gives meaning and significance to experience since it fixes what was done or left undone, and so commands responsibility.

Turning now to the yin trigrams, the primary one is the Receptive:

*K'UN*, The Receptive:

The susceptibility of the world that makes action possible.

In other words, the world is affected by what we do, though not necessarily according to our expectations, desires, or intentions. It is this quality that makes it an arena in which to test power and learn responsibility.

For the three lesser yin trigrams, we can write:

*SUN*, The Wood or Wind:

The integrity of the world which is maintained despite the seeker's actions.

*LI*, The Fire, Clarity:

The lawfulness of the world, independent of the seeker's understanding or acceptance.

*TUI*, The Joyous:

The continuity of the world as the past flows into the present and becomes the future.

This completes the trigrams in the Outer position. Before considering the Inner Nuclear and the Outer Nuclear positions, we need to examine their relation to the Inner and Outer trigrams and to each other. These relations are discussed in the next section.

# STRUCTURAL RELATIONS

The trigrams in the four positions are intimately connected through a system of structural relations. Consider, for example, the Inner and Inner Nuclear trigrams in a hexagram. The former consists of the first, second, and third lines, the latter the second, third, and fourth lines. The second and third lines of a hexagram are, therefore, common to the trigrams in the two positions. The first line is unique to the trigram in the Inner position, the fourth line to that in the Inner Nuclear position. If we specify the trigram in the Inner Nuclear position, the first line can still be either solid or broken, leading to two Inner trigrams. Similarly, if we specify the trigram in the Inner position, the fourth line can be either solid or broken, leading to two Inner Nuclear trigrams. Therefore, either of two Inner trigrams can coexist with either of two Inner Nuclear trigrams.

Similar relations hold between successive positions in the sequence Inner, Inner Nuclear, Outer Nuclear, and Outer.

# THE NUCLEAR TRIGRAMS

The nuclear trigrams (lines 2, 3, and 4 for the Inner Nuclear, and 3, 4, and 5 for the Outer Nuclear) are quite closely related to the Inner trigram (lines 1, 2, and 3) and the Outer trigram (lines 4, 5, and 6). Structurally, this is reflected in the degree of overlap between the trigrams. However, there is also an overlap of significance. The structural relation can be of great help in seeking to understand the roles and meanings of the nuclear trigrams. To illustrate, the Inner trigram and the Inner Nuclear trigram have lines 2 and 3 in common. Suppose we fix those two lines. The inner trigram has line 1 underneath which can be either solid or broken. Hence there are two Inner trigrams that have the given lines 2 and 3. The Inner Nuclear Trigram also has line 4 above the two given lines, and it can also be either solid or broken.

Therefore, there are two possible Inner Nuclear Trigrams that contain the given lines.

As a specific example, suppose the second line is solid, the third broken. Figure 3 shows the possibilities.

Figure 3

SECOND LINE SOLID,
THIRD LINE BROKEN

| | | The Arousal | The Fire |
|---|---|---|---|
| Inner Nuclear Trigram | #4 | ▬ ▬ | ▬▬▬ |
| | #3 | ▬ ▬ | ▬ ▬ |
| | #2 | ▬▬▬ | ▬▬▬ |
| Inner Trigram | #3 | ▬ ▬ | ▬ ▬ |
| | #2 | ▬▬▬ | ▬▬▬ |
| | #1 | ▬ ▬ | ▬▬▬ |
| | | The Abyss | The Joyous |

Similar relations hold for all values of lines #2 and #3. By the study of these possibilities, the student can gain insight into the relations between the meanings of the Inner Nuclear and Inner trigrams.

Similar structural relations also occur between the Outer Nuclear and Outer Trigrams, where the common elements are lines #4 and #5. Again, study of these relations can greatly help the analysis of the relation between the two trigrams.

A similar relation exists between the Inner Nuclear and Outer Nuclear trigram, based on the shared lines, #3 and #4. This structural relation is not as readily translated into the relationship of the meanings, yet it should not be ignored. In particular, it may come into play when a hexagram is being read directly in answer to a question. It is often the case that the Inner Nuclear trigram refers to karmic factors that are at play, and which are represented by the Inner trigram. Those factors are opposed by the situation represented by the Outer trigram. That situation, however, is a reflection of a deeper principle named in the Inner Nuclear trigram. The interplay between the karmic problem and the underlying principles of reality is, then expressed as the relation between the Inner Nuclear and the Outer Nuclear trigrams. It is this relationship that offers the querant the opportunity to gain insight to the karmic problem.

## THE INNER NUCLEAR TRIGRAMS

The Inner Nuclear trigrams identify the inner source of the intention, or the state of mind, of the shaman and priest as they face their problems—i.e., the source of the condition identified by the Inner trigram.

There are many levels on which we can look for the inner source. These can range from the subconscious levels of Freud to the deepest spiritual considerations. In the following, we use the viewpoint of human beings as spiritual entities who seek incarnate existence to acquire experience. The goal of spiritual entities, then, is to understand what is responsibility, and what it means to make a decision and endure the consequences. To realize this objective, the entities must find conditions that make experience useful. Therefore, they knowingly accept the limitations of incarnate existence, for it is only there that they can know the consequences of what they do.

The various aspects of these intentions and conditions are symbolized by the Inner Nuclear trigrams.

The discussion of the interpretations of the Inner Nuclear trigrams is organized according to the structural relations. In effect, we will examine what may be called the Inner tetragrams, lines 1, 2, 3, and 4 in a hexagram.

## SECOND AND THIRD LINES SOLID

If the second and third lines are both solid, the Inner Nuclear trigram is either the *Creative* or the *Joyous*, and the Inner trigram is either again the Creative or the Wood. Considering first the Creative, we can write:

*CH'IEN*, The Creative:

**The intention to experience.**

The intention to experience is a necessary basis for the shaman's exercise of will. Why else should the seeker take the role of the shaman with all the risks that are involved? Also, the intention to experience implies the need to participate in an environment, and the subordination of self to that environment—the aspect symbolized by the trigram Sun, the Wood, in the Inner position. The other Inner Nuclear trigram of the pair is the Joyous:

*TUI*, The Joyous:

**The principle of assimilation.**

The seeker takes the role of the shaman in order to assimilate experience—there would be no point in incarnating if the entity were not willing to make experience its own. Also, the desire to assimilate experience leads to the need for participation, for experience is not likely to be assimilated unless the individual truly feels a part of incarnate existence.

## SECOND LINE BROKEN, THIRD LINE SOLID

In this case, the Inner Nuclear trigram is either the *Abyss* or the *Wood*, and the Inner trigram the *Mountain* or the *Fire*. Considering first the Abyss:

*K'AN*, The Abyss:

**The intention to experience control.**

The experience of control would be empty, without meaning, were its consequences reversible.

Therefore, for the intention to be satisfied, the environment must be one with closure, so that control is achieved through ending, or destruction—the Inner trigram of the Mountain. Further, for control to be exercised, the actor must be able to perceive the variety of his or her environment, and to distinguish the things and changes that occur—the Inner trigram of the Fire.

*SUN*, The Wood or Wind:

The principle of involvement.

The seeker must accept personal involvement with his or her environment, acknowledging participation with it. Otherwise, the power of termination would be empty, for the seeker would have no concern with what is ended. Hence this trigram in the Inner Nuclear position relates directly to the Mountain in the Inner position.

Also, the seeker must acknowledge involvement with his or her environment to perceive the separate things and processes within it. Conversely, by perception, seekers know their own involvement as they recognize that they are some of the distinguishable elements in it, and that their actions are distinguishable processes. Hence the relation to the trigram of the Fire in the Inner position.

## SECOND LINE SOLID, THIRD LINE BROKEN

In this case, the Inner Nuclear trigram is either the *Arousal* or the *Fire*, the Inner trigram either the *Abyss* or the *Joyous*.

Considering first the Arousal:

*CHÊN*, The Arousal:

The intention to experience origination.

To originate, the seeker must exercise some measure of control—therefore the connection to the Abyss in the Inner position. He or she must also be willing to accept the reality of the environment, or origination is nothing more than a dream or fantasy. Hence the connection to the Joyous in the Inner position.

*LI*, The Fire or Clarity:

The principle of discrimination.

The principle of discrimination underlies control. Without the ability to discriminate among the separate things and processes of our environment, there can be no control. Hence the connection to the Abyss in the Inner position. Also, discrimination gives meaning to acceptance. Otherwise, acceptance would mean that the seeker was immersed in an undifferentiated sea of existence, and experience could be no more than the stimulus-response conditioning of reflexes. Hence the connection to the Joyous in the Inner position.


## SECOND AND THIRD LINES BROKEN

Finally, if both lines are broken, the Inner Nuclear trigram is either the *Mountain* or the *Receptive*, the Inner trigram either the *Arousal* or again the *Receptive*.

We consider first the Mountain:

*KÊN*, The Mountain:

The intention to experience finality.

Finality is experienced through the power to initiate. What is ended is replaced by something new, even if the new is simply a vacuum. Indeed, the stress of termination is often due to uncertainty about what will follow. Hence the connection to the Arousal in the Inner position.

The seeker, in fulfilling the intention to experience finality, must take the role of the priest, for he or she cannot know what will be the full consequences of his or her act. Hence the connection to the Receptive in the Inner position.

*K'UN*, The Receptive:

**The principle of reality.**

By this is meant that the seeker must accept the strictures of reality—what he or she does can only be what the conditions of the world make possible. This principle applies in particular to the seeker's intentions to originate—hence the connection to the Arousal in the Inner position.

It is also a part of the reality of the world that the seeker can never know the fullness of that reality. He or she cannot know with certainty or precision what is possible, or what will be the consequences of any event or action. Therefore, the seeker takes the role of the priest, recognizing his or her own subordination to a greater reality. It is this that forms the connection to the Receptive in the Inner position.

This, then completes the system of trigrams in the Inner Nuclear position.

# THE OUTER NUCLEAR TRIGRAMS

Finally, we can analyze the Outer Nuclear trigrams in a similar way. In this position, the trigrams identify those characteristics of reality that create the qualities named in the Outer trigram—qualities that make experience possible and shape its impact. The Outer Nuclear trigrams name the source of those qualities.

It is convenient, again, to organize the analysis with the structural relations between the Outer trigrams and the Outer Nuclear trigrams, and, in effect, consider the sets of tetragrams that share the fourth and fifth lines of a hexagram.

## FOURTH AND FIFTH LINES SOLID

If both these lines are solid, the Outer Nuclear trigram is either the *Creative* or the *Wood*, and the Outer trigram is either the *Creative* or the *Joyous*.

We consider first the Creative in the Outer Nuclear position:

*CH'IEN*, The Creative:

### The principle of autonomy.

The principle of autonomy gives the world its imminence. What happens is not limited by the seeker's desires or expectations, or even by his or her understanding. It is this that provides the link to the Creative in the Outer position.

The world's autonomy is also what makes possible its continuity—symbolized by the Joyous in the Outer position. Evolving according to its own rules, independent of the seeker or his or her expectations or desires, its reality flows out of its history and provides the basis of its future.

### *SUN*, The Wood or Wind:

### The principle of self-consistency.

The world is ever self-consistent. It is this quality that is the basis of the world's imminence, symbolized by the Creative in the Outer position. Moving according to its own consistency rather than the seeker's desires or expectations, it impacts him or her in ways that the seeker may find unexpected and overwhelming.

The world's self-consistency is also the basis for its continuity—symbolized by the Joyous in the Outer position. It is the principle of consistency that links events together and allows influence to weave the parts into a single whole.

## FOURTH LINE BROKEN, FIFTH SOLID

In this case, the Outer Nuclear trigram is either the *Mountain* or the *Fire*, the Outer trigram either the *Abyss* or the *Wood*. Considering first the Mountain:

**KÊN, The Mountain:**

The principle of finality.

The principle of finality gives significance to the flux of change, symbolized by the Abyss in the Outer position, ensuring that the past cannot be changed. In addition, it ensures the integrity of the world, symbolized by the Wood in the Inner position, as it closes off the present from direct influence by the past.

*LI*, The Fire or Clarity:

The principle of lawfulness.

The principle of lawfulness governs the flux of change within the world, symbolized by the Abyss in the Inner position. Otherwise, change would be chaos. The principle is also manifested in the world's integrity, symbolized by the Wood in the Outer position; the world's integrity is the visible expression of its Law.

## FOURTH LINE SOLID, FIFTH BROKEN

Here, the Outer Nuclear trigram is either the *Abyss* or the *Joyous*, and the Outer trigram is either the *Arousal* or the *Fire*. Considering first the Abyss, we obtain the following:

*K'AN*, The Abyss:

The principle of change.

The principle of change asserts that nothing in the world remains unchanging, even for an instant. This ensures the world's unpredictability, symbolized by the Arousal in the Outer position. Yet change would be chaos except for the world's lawfulness, symbolized by the Fire in the Outer position.

*TUI*, The Joyous:

The principle of comprehensibility.

This somewhat awkward phrase is meant to name the aspect of the world that permits us, as seekers, to comprehend it in part, even if we cannot ever understand it fully. Despite the errors and incompleteness of our understanding, we are able to use what we do understand, and to seek to perfect what we think we know.

As stated, we cannot ever understand reality in its entirety or with complete precision. Therefore, the world remains unpredictable—as symbolized by the Arousal in the Outer position. The partial understanding that we can reach, and which is a consequence of the principle, approximates the Law we cannot know and so makes useful the lawfulness of the world that is symbolized by the Fire in the Outer position.

## FOURTH AND FIFTH LINES BROKEN

In the last case, the Outer Nuclear trigram is either the *Arousal* or the *Receptive*, the Outer trigram either the *Mountain* or the *Receptive*. Considering first the Arousal:

*CHEN*, The Arousal:

The principle of uniqueness.

This principle asserts that the world is ever new, ever unique. Therefore, the past is closed and the closure of finality pervades existence as symbolized by the Mountain in the Outer position. The uniqueness of the world also allows for its susceptibility, symbolized by the Receptive in the Outer position. The world recreates itself in each instant of its becoming, and so can be susceptible to what the seeker does or chooses not to do.

*K'UN*, The Receptive:

**The principle of potentiation.**

The principle asserts the unboundedness of possibility as the world recreates itself in each instant. Before the new is manifested, it exists within the potentiation of the Void. The existential world is born from what exists in potentiality within essentiality.

The finality of the world—symbolized by the Mountain in the Outer position—makes it possible to experience potentiality. It allows what has served its time to disappear so that what comes to be can be recognized. It also makes possible the world's susceptibility—symbolized by the Mountain in the Outer position.

This completes the listing of the Outer Nuclear trigrams and their links to the Outer trigrams.

## CONCLUSIONS

The results of this analysis are summarized in Table 3 in Chapter VI. There, we have isolated significant words and phrases from the above as keys to the trigrams in the various positions. The logic behind these keys, however, as well as what we mean by them, is that given above. It is this logic and meaning that is used in the interpretations of the hexagrams in Chapter VII and Chapter VIII.

# CHAPTER X

# HEXAGRAM TABLES

The following tables provide a number of cross-reference tables which are useful. First, Table 4 shows the full sequence of the hexagrams in their conventional order that King Wen is thought to have originated and the principle translations of the Chinese names as given in the Wilhelm/Baynes translation.

Table 5 provides an alphabetical listing from the Chinese name (again as given in the Wilhelm/Baynes translation), to English and the numbers of the hexagrams.

Table 6 lists in alphabetical order the English names to the hexagram numbers.

Finally, Table 7 shows the Chinese pronunciation of the names of the trigrams and hexagrams.

## Table 4

| THE SEQUENCE OF HEXAGRAMS | | |
|---|---|---|
| 1 | Ch'ien | The Creative |
| 2 | K'un | The Receptive |
| 3 | Chun | Difficulty at the Beginning |
| 4 | Mêng | Youthful Folly |
| 5 | Hsü | Waiting |
| 6 | Sung | Conflict |
| 7 | Shih | The Army |
| 8 | Pi | Holding Together |
| 9 | Hsiao Ch'u | The Taming Power of the Small |
| 10 | Lü | Treading |
| 11 | T'ai | Peace |
| 12 | P'i | Standstill |
| 13 | T'ung Jên | Fellowship with Men |
| 14 | Ta Yu | Possession in Great Measure |
| 15 | Ch'ien | Modesty |
| 16 | Yü | Enthusiasm |
| 17 | Sui | Following |
| 18 | Ku | Work on What Has Been Spoiled |
| 19 | Lin | Approach |
| 20 | Kuan | Contemplation |
| 21 | Shih Ho | Biting Through |
| 22 | Pi | Grace |

## Table 4 (Continued)

| THE SEQUENCE OF HEXAGRAMS | | |
|---|---|---|
| 23 | Po | Splitting Apart |
| 24 | Fu | Return |
| 25 | Wu Wang | Innocence |
| 26 | Ta Ch'u | The Taming Power of the Great |
| 27 | I | The Corners of the Mouth |
| 28 | Ta Kuo | Preponderance of the Great |
| 29 | K'an | The Abysmal |
| 30 | Li | Fire |
| 31 | Hsien | Influence |
| 32 | Hêng | Duration |
| 33 | Tun | Retreat |
| 34 | Ta Chuang | The Power of the Great |
| 35 | Chin | Progress |
| 36 | Ming I | Darkening of the Light |
| 37 | Chia Jên | The Family |
| 38 | K'uei | Opposition |
| 39 | Chien | Obstruction |
| 40 | Hsieh | Deliverance |
| 41 | Sun | Decrease |
| 42 | I | Increase |
| 43 | Kuai | Breakthrough |
| 44 | Kou | Coming to Meet |

Table 4 (Continued)

## THE SEQUENCE OF HEXAGRAMS

| 45 | *Ts'ui* | Gathering Together |
|----|---------|--------------------|
| 46 | *Shêng* | Pushing Upward |
| 47 | *K'un* | Oppression |
| 48 | *Ching* | The Well |
| 49 | *Ko* | Revolution |
| 50 | *Ting* | The Caldron |
| 51 | *Chên* | The Arousing |
| 52 | *Kên* | Keeping Still |
| 53 | *Chien* | Development |
| 54 | *Kuei Mei* | The Marrying Maiden |
| 55 | *Fêng* | Abundance |
| 56 | *Lü* | The Wanderer |
| 57 | *Sun* | The Gentle |
| 58 | *Tui* | The Joyous |
| 59 | *Huan* | Dispersion |
| 60 | *Chieh* | Limitation |
| 61 | *Chung Fu* | Inner Truth |
| 62 | *Hsiao Kuo* | Preponderance of the Small |
| 63 | *Chi Chi* | After Completion |
| 64 | *Wei Chi* | Before Completion |

## Table 5

| CHINESE NAME TO ENGLISH TO NUMBER | | |
|---|---|---|
| *Chên* | The Arousing | 51 |
| *Chi Chi* | After Completion | 63 |
| *Chia Jên* | The Family | 37 |
| *Chieh* | Limitation | 60 |
| *Ch'ien* | The Creative | 1 |
| *Ch'ien* | Modesty | 15 |
| *Chien* | Obstruction | 39 |
| *Chien* | Development | 53 |
| *Chin* | Progress | 35 |
| *Ching* | The Well | 48 |
| *Chun* | Difficulty at the Beginning | 3 |
| *Chung Fu* | Inner Truth | 61 |
| *Fêng* | Abundance | 55 |
| *Fu* | Return | 24 |
| *Hêng* | Duration | 32 |
| *Hsiao Ch'u* | The Taming Power of the Small | 9 |
| *Hsiao Kuo* | Preponderance of the Small | 62 |
| *Hsieh* | Deliverance | 40 |
| *Hsien* | Influence | 31 |
| *Hsü* | Waiting | 5 |

Note: The transliterated names of some of the hexagrams are identical. however, the Chinese characters are quite different, and the apparent duplication should not cause confusion.

## Table 5 (Continued)

| CHINESE NAME TO ENGLISH TO NUMBER | | |
|---|---|---|
| Huan | Dispersion | 59 |
| I | The Corners of the Mouth | 27 |
| I | Increase | 42 |
| K'an | The Abysmal | 29 |
| Kên | Keeping Still | 52 |
| Ko | Revolution | 49 |
| Kou | Coming to Meet | 44 |
| K'uei | Opposition | 38 |
| Kuei Mei | The Marrying Maiden | 54 |
| K'un | The Receptive | 2 |
| K'un | Oppression | 47 |
| Ku | Work on What Has Been Spoiled | 18 |
| Kuai | Breakthrough | 43 |
| Kuan | Contemplation | 20 |
| Li | Fire | 30 |
| Lin | Approach | 19 |
| Lü | Treading | 10 |
| Lü | The Wanderer | 56 |
| Mêng | Youthful Folly | 4 |
| Ming I | Darkening of the Light | 36 |
| Pi | Holding Together | 8 |
| Pi | Grace | 22 |

## Table 5 (Continued)

| CHINESE NAME TO ENGLISH TO NUMBER | | |
|---|---|---|
| P'i | Standstill | 12 |
| Po | Splitting Apart | 23 |
| Shêng | Pushing Upward | 46 |
| Shih | The Army | 7 |
| Shih Ho | Biting Through | 21 |
| Sui | Following | 17 |
| Sun | Decrease | 41 |
| Sun | The Gentle | 57 |
| Sung | Conflict | 6 |
| Ta Ch'u | The Taming Power of the Great | 26 |
| Ta Chuang | The Power of the Great | 34 |
| Ta Kuo | Preponderance of the Great | 28 |
| T'ai | Peace | 11 |
| Ting | The Caldron | 50 |
| Ta Yu | Possession in Great Measure | 14 |
| Ts'ui | Gathering Together | 45 |
| Tui | The Joyous | 58 |
| Tun | Retreat | 33 |
| T'ung Jên | Fellowship with Men | 13 |
| Wei Chi | Before Completion | 64 |
| Wu Wang | Innocence | 25 |
| Yü | Enthusiasm | 16 |

## Table 6

| ENGLISH NAME TO NUMBER | |
|---|---|
| Abundance | 55 |
| Abysmal, The | 29 |
| After Completion | 63 |
| Approach | 19 |
| Army, The | 7 |
| Arousing, The | 51 |
| Before Completion | 64 |
| Beginning, Difficulty at the | 3 |
| Biting Through | 21 |
| Breakthrough | 43 |
| Caldron, The | 50 |
| Clan, The | 37 |
| Clinging, The | 30 |
| Coming to Meet | 44 |
| Completion, After | 63 |
| Completion, Before | 64 |
| Conflict | 6 |
| Contemplation | 20 |
| Corners of the Mouth, The | 27 |
| Creative, The | 1 |
| Darkening of the Light | 36 |
| Decay | 18 |

## Table 6 (Continued)

| ENGLISH NAME TO NUMBER | |
|---|---|
| Decrease | 41 |
| Deliverance | 40 |
| Development | 53 |
| Difficulty at the Beginning | 3 |
| Dispersion | 59 |
| Dissolution | 59 |
| Duration | 32 |
| Enthusiasm | 16 |
| Exhaustion | 47 |
| Family, The | 37 |
| Fellowship with Men | 13 |
| Fire, The | 30 |
| Following | 17 |
| Fullness | 55 |
| Gathering Together | 45 |
| Gentle, The | 57 |
| Grace | 22 |
| Gradual Progress | 53 |
| Great Measure, Possession in | 14 |
| Great, Preponderance of the | 28 |
| Great, Taming Power of the | 26 |
| Holding Together | 8 |

## Table 6 (Continued)

| ENGLISH NAME TO NUMBER | |
|---|---|
| Increase | 42 |
| Influence | 31 |
| Inner Truth | 61 |
| Innocence | 25 |
| Joyous, The | 58 |
| Keeping Still | 52 |
| Lake, The | 58 |
| Light, Darkening of the | 36 |
| Limitation | 60 |
| Maiden, The Marrying | 54 |
| Massing | 45 |
| Meet, Coming to | 44 |
| Men, Fellowship with | 13 |
| Modesty | 15 |
| Molting | 49 |
| Mountain, The | 52 |
| Mouth, The Corners of the | 27 |
| Nourishment | 5 |
| Obstruction | 39 |
| Opposition | 38 |
| Oppression | 47 |
| Peace | 11 |

## Table 6 (Continued)

| ENGLISH NAME TO NUMBER | |
|---|---|
| Penetrating, The | 57 |
| Possession in Great Measure | 14 |
| Power of the Great, The | 34 |
| Power of the Great, The Taming | 26 |
| Preponderance of the Great | 28 |
| Preponderance of the Small | 62 |
| Progress | 35 |
| Progress, Gradual | 53 |
| Pushing Upward | 46 |
| Receptive, The | 2 |
| Resoluteness | 43 |
| Retreat | 33 |
| Return | 24 |
| Revolution | 49 |
| Shock | 51 |
| Small, The Taming Power of the | 9 |
| Small, Preponderance of the | 62 |
| Splitting Apart | 23 |
| Spoiled, Work on What Has Been | 18 |
| Stagnation | 12 |
| Standstill | 12 |
| Taming Power of the Great, The | 26 |

### Table 6 (Continued)

| ENGLISH NAME TO NUMBER | |
|---|---|
| Taming Power of the Small, The | 9 |
| Thunder | 51 |
| Treading | 10 |
| Truth, Inner | 61 |
| Turning Point, The | 24 |
| Unexpected, The | 25 |
| Union | 8 |
| Waiting | 5 |
| Wanderer, The | 56 |
| Water | 29 |
| Well, The | 48 |
| Wind, The | 57 |
| Wooing | 31 |
| Work on What Has Been Spoiled | 18 |
| Youthful Folly | 4 |

# GUIDE TO PRONUNCIATION

The following guide to the pronunciation of the Chinese names of the trigrams and hexagrams is based primarily on material in John Blofeld's *The Book of Change*, published by E. P. Dutton & Co., Inc., New York, 1966. He gives a transcription of the Chinese names that, he says, is both according to the Wade System and to a "rough and ready" system of his own.

One principle that is worth remembering is that the sounds for "T," "Ch," "Ts," and "K" are unvoiced if they are followed by an apostrophe; otherwise they are voiced. Thus "I Ching" is pronounced "Yee Jing" since the "ch" is not followed by an apostrophe. On the other hand, the "ch" in "Ch'ien" is unvoiced, pronounced as in cheek.

(In the order of their occurrence in the sequence of hexagrams)

**Table 7**

| PRONUNCIATION GUIDE | | |
|---|---|---|
| 1. *CH'IEN* | The Creative | "chee'en" |
| 2. *K'UN* | The Receptive | "kwen," the "e" almost silent. |
| 3. *CHUN* | Difficulty at the Beginning | "jwen," the "e" almost silent. |
| 4. *MÊNG* | Youthful Folly | "meng," the "e" almost silent. |
| 5. *HSÜ* | Waiting | "shu," the "u" rhyming with the french "tu" |
| 6. *SUNG* | Conflict | "soong" |
| 7. *SHIH* | The Army | "shrrr" |
| 8. *PI* | Holding Together | "bee" |

## Table 7 (Continued)

| PRONUNCATION GUIDE | | |
| --- | --- | --- |
| 9. *HSAIO CH'U* | The Taming Power of the Small | "she-au choo," the "au" as in "house." |
| 10. *LÜ* | Treading | "lu" rhyming with the French "tu" |
| 11. *T'AI* | Peace | "tie," as in "necktie." |
| 12. *P'I* | Standstill | "pee" |
| 13. *T'UNG JÊN* | Fellowship with Men | "toong ren," the "e" silent. |
| 14. *TA YU* | Possession in Great Measure | "dah you" |
| 15. *CH'IEN* | Modesty | "chee-en" |
| 16. *YÜ* | Enthusiasm | "yu," rhyming with the French "tu" |
| 17. *SUI* | Following | "sway" |
| 18. *KU* | Work on What Has Been Spoiled | "goo" |
| 19. *LIN* | Approach | "lin" |
| 20. *KUAN* | Contemplation | "gwun," rhyming with "done." |
| 21. *SHIH HO* | Biting Through | "shrrr he," the "he" as in "her" with the "r" silent. |
| 22. *PI* | Grace | "bee" |
| 23. *PO* | Splitting Apart | "po," a short "o." |
| 24. *FU* | Return | "foo" |

## Table 7  (Continued)

| PRONUNCIATION GUIDE | | |
|---|---|---|
| 25. *WU WANG* | Innocence | "woo wung" |
| 26. *TA CH'U* | The Taming Power of the Small | "dah choo" |
| 27. *I* | The Corners of the Mouth | "yee" |
| 28. *TA KUO* | Preponderance of the Great | "dah gwo," with a short "o." |
| 29. *K'AN* | The Abysmal | cun, as in "cunning." |
| 30. *LI* | Fire | "lee" |
| 31. *HSIEN* | Influence | "shee-en" |
| 32. *HÊNG* | Duration | "heng," the "e" almost silent. |
| 33. *TUN* | Retreat | "doon," with the "oo" as in "book." |
| 34. *TA CHUANG* | The Power of the Great | "dah jwung," rhyming with "hung." |
| 35. *CHIN* | Progress | "jin" |
| 36. *MING I* | Darkening of the Light | "ming yee" |
| 37. *CHIA JÊN* | The Family | "jee-ah ren," the "e" in "ren" almost silent. |
| 38. *K'UEI* | Opposition | "kway" |
| 39. *CHIEN* | Obstruction | "jee-en" |
| 40. *HSIEH* | Deliverance | "shee-ay," rhyming with "hay." |

### Table 7  (Continued)

| PRONUNCATION GUIDE | | |
|---|---|---|
| 41. *SUN* | Decrease | "soon," the "oo" as in "book." |
| 42. *I* | Increase | "yee" |
| 43. *KUAI* | Breakthrough | "guy" |
| 44. *KOU* | Coming to Meet | "go" |
| 45. *TS'UI* | Gathering Together | "tsway" |
| 46. *SHÊNG* | Pushing Upward | "sheng," the "e" almost silent. |
| 47. *K'UN* | Oppression | "kwen," the "e" almost silent. |
| 48. *CHING* | The Well | "jing" |
| 49. *KO* | Revolution | "ge," with a short "e." |
| 50. *TING* | The Caldron | "ding" |
| 51. *CHÊN* | The Arousing | "jen," the "e" almost silent. |
| 52. *KÊN* | Keeping Still | "gen," the "e" almost silent. |
| 53. *CHIEN* | Development | "jee-en" |
| 54. *KUEI MEI* | Marrying Maiden | "gway may" |
| 55. *FÊNG* | Abundance | "feng," the "e" almost silent. |
| 56. *LÜ* | The Wanderer | lu, rhyming with the French "tu" |
| 57. *SUN* | The Wood | "soon," the "oo" as in "book." |

## Table 7  (Continued)

| PRONUNCATION GUIDE | | |
|---|---|---|
| 58. *TUI* | The Joyous | "dway" |
| 59. *HINAN* | Dispersion | "hwun," rhyming with "done." |
| 60. *CHIEH* | Limitation | "jee-eh" |
| 61. *CHUNG FU* | Inner Truth | "joong foo" |
| 62. *HSIAO KUO* | Preponderance of the Small | "shee-au gwo," with the "o" short. |
| 63. *CHI CHI* | After Completion | "jee jee" |
| 64. *WEI CHI* | Before Completion | "way jee" |

# GLOSSARY

The first section lists and briefly defines the terms used in the I Ching. These terms are defined in more detail in the main text; the definitions given here are intended only to remind the reader. The section General Terms lists and briefly defines other terms used in the text. Again, the definitions are not complete and are no substitute for sources that discuss the concepts more extensively. However, they may be of help to readers who have not been deeply involved with the relevant concepts.

## TERMS USED WITH THE I CHING

CASTING THE ORACLE. An expression for the process of throwing the coins or using some other technique to develop what is called the primary hexagram in response to a question. In the coin technique, three coins are thrown simultaneously six times. Each throw determines the nature of one line in the hexagram— i.e., whether it is solid or broken, changing or not. Note: The lines are determined and numbered from the bottom up. That is, the first throw of the coins determines the bottom line of the hexagram, the second throw the next line, and so on until the sixth throw determines the top line.

CHANGING LINE. Changing lines, if any, are determined during the process of casting the oracle as discussed in Chapter I. If a line is changing, it is changed when the secondary hexagram is developed from the primary one. If the line is originally solid it becomes broken, if originally broken it becomes solid.

DUKE of CHOU. Son of King Wen and the author of the earliest available text on the individual lines in the hexagrams.

FAMILY ARRANGEMENT.   The arrangement and classification of the eight possible trigrams shown in Table 2. The trigrams are identified as "father" and "mother" plus three "sons" and three "daughters." The arrangement offers an interpretation of the trigrams that is thought to have originated with King Wen around 1150 B.C.

HEXAGRAM.   A symbol composed of six lines, each of which can be either solid or broken. There are sixty-four distinct hexagrams.

I CHING.   "Book of Change" or "Book of Changes." The Chinese language does not distinguish between these two translations, but either is appropriate.

INNER NUCLEAR TRIGRAM.   Lines 2, 3, and 4 in a hexagram, counting from the bottom. This trigram is interpreted as indicating the origin of the questioner's state as identified in the inner trigram. The inner nuclear trigram can be said to describe what "lies behind" the inner trigram and the querrant's question—what consideration or condition or past history of the questioner has led him or her to find a problem in the situation.

INNER TRIGRAM.   Lines 1, 2, and 3 (the bottom three lines) in a hexagram. This trigram is understood as representing the questioner, or the person or group in whose behalf the question is being asked.

KING WEN.   The author of the earliest available text on the hexagrams. He wrote this text around 1150 B.C. and is generally credited with originating the family arrangement of the trigrams.

LINE.   A symbol that may have either of two values. If it is a "solid" line, it is represented as " ▬▬▬ "; if a "broken" one, it is shown as " ▬▬ ▬▬ ." Each throw of the coins generates one line which may, in addition, be either "changing" or not.

*LING*.   A Chinese word naming the ability to use the I Ching. *Ling* is generally recognized as having two parts. The first is the ability to cast the oracle and obtain a meaningful answer. The second is the ability to see what that answer has to do with the question— i.e., to see why the answer is an answer. Note that the first part concerns the mechanics of the oracle, the second explicitly requires intuition.

OUTER NUCLEAR TRIGRAM.   Lines 3, 4, and 5 (counting from the bottom) in a hexagram. This trigram can be said to represent what has led to the situation named in the outer trigram. In a sense, it identifies what "lies behind" the situation that is a problem for the questioner.

OUTER TRIGRAM.   Lines 4, 5, and 6 (the top three lines) of a hexagram. This trigram is understood as representing the source of the questioner's problem, be it another person or group, a real-world situation, whatever. In any case, it is external to the questioner as the latter is represented in the inner trigram.

PRIMARY HEXAGRAM.   The hexagram actually obtained by casting the oracle. Some of these lines may be changing.

SECONDARY HEXAGRAM.   The hexagram obtained from the primary one by changing all the changing lines, assuming there are some. No lines in the secondary hexagram are considered changing. If there are no changing lines in the primary hexagram, the secondary hexagram is the same as the primary one. Since none, any, or all of the lines in the primary hexagram can be changing, a primary hexagram can change into any hexagram. However, the probabilities are that any given cast of the oracle will result in a primary hexagram with not more than two or three lines changing.

TEN WINGS.   A series of commentaries on the I Ching written around the 9th century B.C. either by Confucius or by his disciples and attributed to him. They have become part of the canonical literature of the I Ching.

TRIGRAM.   A set of three lines, each of which can be solid or broken. Since each line has two possibilities, there are eight different trigrams. A hexagram can be viewed as primarily composed of two trigrams, one above the other called the "inner" and "outer" trigrams.

# GENERAL TERMS

AKASHIC RECORDS.   According to many, there is a level of awareness at which all things, past present or future, are recorded. Those who are able to access to this level to any significant degree are said "to consult the Akashic records."

ARCHETYPE.   According to C. G. Jung, archetypes are the basis of thought and consciousness generated from the collective experiences of humanity. They provide the foundation for all cognition and so operate at a deeper level than language or even thought. Hence they remain essentially indefinable in full, beyond rational analysis or discussion, although we can sometimes identify some of their contents.

BODHISATTVA.   In Buddhism, a Bodhisattva is one who reaches the threshold of Buddhahood but turns back from that final step in order to serve mankind.

DIVINATION.   The practice of seeking answers to problems through methods that are outside the normal modes of analysis or perception. These methods generally use some device or ritual but still depend fundamentally on intuition.

KARMA.   In its simplest form, karma is the idea that actions, good or bad, are compensated either later in a person's life or in a succeeding life. A variant view is that the person who performs an action, be it good or bad, needs to understand the full nature and consequences of what he or she has done. If that understanding is not immediately present or is incomplete, then variations on the situation will be encountered in the person's current life or another one until full understanding is reached.

KARMIC PURPOSE.   This phrase is based on the idea that we, as spiritual entities, chose to become incarnate in the material world under specific circumstances in order to address some particular problem or problems that are the residues of experiences and actions in past lives. A karmic purpose thus becomes the main theme of a given life.

LINEAR INCARNATION.   The belief that we are spiritual entities that incarnate in one body after another but only one at a time. Presumably, the purpose is to learn and become through experience. The alternative view is that we incarnate as individuals from a spiritual entity that is not limited to one incarnation at a time. The latter view might be called "multilinear incarnation."

RESPONSIBILITY.   Literally, the ability to respond. In turn, "to respond" comes from the Latin, *re* + *spondere*, to promise back. Therefore responsibility is the willingness and ability to learn from present experience and to change those patterns of actions that have been shown to be in error or inappropriate. Responsibility is not guilt. Indeed, guilt often blocks the ability to acknowledge error, and so becomes an obstacle to the true acceptance of responsibility.

SYNCHRONICITY.   A concept originated by C. G. Jung to explain how apparently unrelated events can influence each other. In brief, events are understood as arising out of the total context in which they occur, making possible various subtle and unidentifiable connections that can lead to their being related in ways that are often dismissed as mere coincidence. The opposite view sees the world as "causal" or "linear" with each event essentially arising from one or a few preceding causes. In fact, both views are important elements of life. The West has tended to emphasize the causal point of view, the East the synchronous one. The viewpoint of the I Ching can best be described as based on synchronicity.

TAO.   Pronounced "Dow" and sometimes translated as "The Way." The Tao is the basic concept of Taoism, one of the major religions of the East dating from about 900 B.C. The central idea is that those who know the Tao remain ever in harmony with the reality in which they move, and so do what serves without effort or confusion.

YIN/YANG.   In Taoism, the basic duality of the world of experience. Yin is receptive, acceptive, compliant, responsive, nurturing, etc. Yang is active, intentional, causative, decisive, creative, etc. In considering flows of influence, the origin of the flow is the yang pole, the person or thing influenced is the yin pole of the flow. Yin is normally identified as feminine, Yang as masculine. A false dichotomy that is sometimes expressed is to see yin as bad or even evil, yang as good. This is counter to pure Taoism, however. To be yang when the situation calls for a yin response is bad, inharmonious; so is it to be yin when the situation needs the yang response. In either case, the Tao has been lost. Both are good, therefore, when used appropriately, and both are bad when misapplied. The words *Yin* and *Yang* originated with Taoism, some 200 years after King Wen. However, when his texts speak of a line being strong or light, the meaning is essentially that of the Yang principle. When he speaks of a weak or dark line, it corresponds to the Yin principle.

Table 8

## KEY TO THE HEXAGRAMS

|  | OUTER | | | | | | | |
|---|---|---|---|---|---|---|---|---|
| **INNER** | ☰ | ☳ | ☵ | ☶ | ☷ | ☴ | ☲ | ☱ |
| ☰ | 1 | 34 | 5 | 26 | 11 | 9 | 14 | 43 |
| ☳ | 25 | 51 | 3 | 27 | 24 | 42 | 21 | 17 |
| ☵ | 6 | 40 | 29 | 4 | 7 | 59 | 64 | 47 |
| ☶ | 33 | 62 | 39 | 52 | 15 | 53 | 56 | 31 |
| ☷ | 12 | 16 | 8 | 23 | 2 | 20 | 35 | 45 |
| ☴ | 44 | 32 | 48 | 18 | 46 | 57 | 50 | 28 |
| ☲ | 13 | 55 | 63 | 22 | 36 | 37 | 30 | 49 |
| ☱ | 10 | 54 | 60 | 41 | 19 | 61 | 38 | 58 |

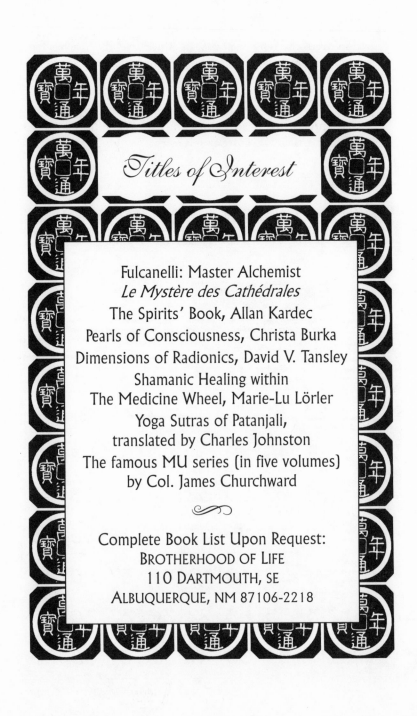

*Titles of Interest*

Fulcanelli: Master Alchemist
*Le Mystère des Cathédrales*
The Spirits' Book, Allan Kardec
Pearls of Consciousness, Christa Burka
Dimensions of Radionics, David V. Tansley
Shamanic Healing within
The Medicine Wheel, Marie-Lu Lörler
Yoga Sutras of Patanjali,
translated by Charles Johnston
The famous MU series (in five volumes)
by Col. James Churchward

Complete Book List Upon Request:
BROTHERHOOD OF LIFE
110 DARTMOUTH, SE
ALBUQUERQUE, NM 87106-2218